I0137620

Man, above of all the
Creatures of earth, can change his
Own pattern. Man above is architect
Of his destiny.
The greatest revolution in our
Generation
Is the discovery that human beings,
By changing the inner attitudes
Of their minds can change the outer

Aspects of their lives.

—William james
Founder of american psychology

Love Secrets

Falling in Love & Staying in Love

Love Secrets

Falling in Love & Staying in Love

Blenda R. Pilon, MSc

© 2017 by Blenda R. Pilon

All rights reserved. No part of this book may be reproduced or transmitted in any form or by any means, electronic or mechanical, including photocopying, recording, or by any information storage and retrieval system, except in the case of brief quotations embodied in critical articles and reviews, without prior written permission of the publisher.

Although the author and publisher have made every effort to ensure the accuracy and completeness of information contained in this book, we assume no responsibility for errors, inaccuracies, omissions, or any inconsistency herein.

ISBN Paperback: 978-9-9762773-8-5
ISBN eBook: 978-9-9762773-9-2

Cover artwork: Amanda Rallings, Yaro Web Design
Interior design: Ghislain Viau

*My heart goes out to all those people who desire to love
and be loved for who they Truly are.*

*I dedicate this book to all those people who want to attract their ideal
partner and enjoy a loving relationship that lasts forever.*

Contents

Chapter One
The Heart of the Matter

Chapter Two
Asking For What You Want

Chapter Three
Six-Week Action Program

Chapter Four
Unmasking Myths

Chapter Five
Love Communication

Chapter Six
Change Your Thoughts, Change Your Relationships

Chapter Seven
A Touch Of Love

Gratitude

With utmost respect, I am grateful for Love that flows through me and is the source of my LOVE POWER. It is my Divine gift that I am deeply honored to share with you.

I am thankful to all those people who desire to make *Falling in Love & Staying in Love* a reality rather than merely a Fairy Tale. You are my inspiration!

With heartfelt gratitude for making *LOVE SECRETS, Falling in Love & Staying in Love* possible, I warmly thank:

My fantastic husband, Rev. Raymond Pilon, whose unconditional loving support and many contributions have made this book possible.

Dr. John Gray, whose endorsement and Love Communication chapter I deeply cherish and value.

My Spiritual God-Son, Glenn Hamilton, for his marketing expertise and continued faith.

For their editorial, professional and moral support; Cat Uhlin, Sy Silverberg, Amanda Rallings, Rev. Carrie Hunter, Dr. Melba Burns, Skip and Denise Rowland, June and Michael White, Julia Markus, Raywyn M.E. Currie, Julianne Pauley, Sarah Lindsey Dickens, Bette Parent, Gwyneth Hart, Sherrel Richards, Misty Klassen and Patsy's darling Multi-poo Mix named Bunny.

Without the help of all my wonderful friends and associates, I could not have written this book!!!

Foreword

From The Author's Husband

Blenda asked me to write the Foreword as a testimony of our lasting relationship/marriage of 25 years. I am deeply grateful to have played a very small part as one of the many editors plus writing the Foreword and closing Love Prayer.

Are you aware that the subject most thoroughly explored in all forms of media is the deep-driving desire for all Human Beings to develop and sustain relationships, be it between parent and child, brother and sister, friends, or between two people who want to share their lives together?

Never before have I met a Human Being with more compassion for other people than Blenda possesses. It was her compassion that created within me the love spark to develop, and now to sustain, a lasting relationship with her - this incredibly loving Human Being.

Blenda does not talk much about this, but I have witnessed miracles in some of the sessions with which I have been privileged to assist her. By miracles, I mean people overcoming long-term problems like fear of intimacy in a matter of one or two sessions. I am talking about clients who had tried, without success, everything medically available to them.

Blenda has created a six week action program based on her seventeen-year private practice and ten plus years of metaphysical training, as well as a masters degree in counselling. This program will put you in touch with that deep sense of self, that missing link that academic and self-help books on the psychology of human relationships talk about. Blenda calls it your LOVE POWER. It is the spiritual *essence,* the common denominator, of all Human Beings. It goes beyond biology, chemistry, medicine, drugs and the physical world. It is the focus of this book.

It has been said that to love someone, you must first love yourself. This program will explore the most important element of relationships. One more thing: be prepared to explore sensitive, painful and dark areas of your inner self. If you do, you will experience a sense of peace, excitement and *Well Being* that you have as yet only imagined.

Please read every sentence at least three times, and then practice what you understand intellectually. It is only through experience that Blenda's techniques will benefit you in your pursuit of a loving, lasting relationship. I am confident that after following Blenda's six-week program faithfully and consistently, you either will have, or will very soon will attract, your perfect lasting relationship

What is our secret to a lasting relationship? I believe it is our desire to always get back to the love, no matter what. Spiritual harmony is our absolute commitment to achieving a loving, fulfilling relationship. Harmony in our relationship is paramount for peace, joy and happiness.

I leave you with this thought: "LOVE POWER is the most powerful force in the Universe – it is God expressing." Trust your faith. What you learn from this program is directly proportional not only to your beliefs, but to becoming the living embodiment of your beliefs. I invite you to have fun.

Rev. Raymond Pilon, CIMM, Canadian International Metaphysical Ministry

Preface

You are precious! Because your success in achieving a loving and lasting relationship is important, I offer you keys for unlocking and discovering your power of Love. With gratitude to the many people who have helped me, I have written *LOVE SECRETS, Falling in Love & Staying in Love.*

For seventeen years I owned and managed a private practice called *Professional Clinical Therapy* specializing in relationship issues. Before I would accept a client, I would ask, "Are you willing to *Expect Success?*" The client's commitment to success changed the energy from struggling to ease. By the time the client arrived, we both held an expectation of success. Fifty percent or more of the work was already accomplished. My job as a relationship therapist was to support my clients in removing relationship barriers and achieving their goals.

Do you believe it is everyone's birthright to be happy and enjoy a loving, lasting relationship? I do! Fortunately I have some knowledge to be of service, and am grateful to share my gifts. I am confident about my six-week action program and believe that as you do your assignments and discover how to use the power of Love, you will fulfill your relationship dreams.

For those of you who are single: I expect that by the end of the program, you will no longer be trying to attract someone special - you will either be selecting the person who is right for you, or will have met your ideal partner.

For those of you who are couples: I expect that by the end of the program, you will have discovered the power of Love that resides within you and will be at ease using your new relationship skills. You will learn that as a Spiritual Being, having a human experience, you can create what you want by thinking correctly. Also, you will be able to listen and to express clearly what you genuinely want, and be valued for the worthwhile person you know in your heart that you are. With the power of your love unleashed, you will experience more joy and laughing, more in-depth discussions, more hugs and kisses, more romantic evenings, more sharing, and a deeper level of intimacy.

What I am telling you reaches beyond the books. Much of what I know comes from my own life. For example, my former husband and I led a large singles club. Our members believed we exemplified the perfect marriage. Unfortunately, my husband and I intuitively knew our marriage was falling apart. When the inevitable happened, I was mystified. I wondered, "What have I done wrong?"

Suddenly finding myself single, alone and scared, I pledged to do whatever it took to create a solid, lasting relationship and then to share what I learned. Believing that a great way to discover what men and women truly want in a relationship is to listen carefully and learn from their experiences, I started up my own private practice. I was dedicated to discovering what makes a true intimate relationship and then to sharing my findings.

As I listened to the stories of my clients, I learned that most men want to please women. Tradition has taught men that *pleasing a woman* is their job, and this is important to feeling loved by their partner. Usually men are more physical than women. Performing well sexually and in their work empowers men to feel worthy of being loved. Men need to be appreciated. For most women to feel worthy of being loved, they want to be nurturers. They also desire their relationship to feel comfortable and emotionally supportive. Women like to be listened to and heard without being criticized or overwhelmed with suggestions. Most women feel loved when they can inspire their partners, when they feel listened to, and when their heart tells them their relationship is working. Like men, they also need to be appreciated.

To be expected, in this fast changing world, what men and women want from relationships is rapidly changing. More than ever before, women want men who are open to expressing their thoughts and feelings and are willing to share. Women want their independence and want to release men from feeling it is their responsibility to please them. Men want women who will take responsibility for helping them be able to express their thoughts and feelings. Men also want women to communicate more specifically what they want, and without hidden agendas. All-in-all, couples want a more authentic, vibrant relationship. Both men and women want more sharing, more fun, more romance and better sex.

In my own personal journey to learn what it takes to achieve a loving, lasting relationship, I discovered I had to go beyond role patterns and what I had learned. For example, I had to let my partners know they meant more to me than just their performance. I had to stop depending on men to support me physically and financially. Perhaps most difficult, I had to change my belief that "in order to feel good, I needed a man to take care of me." This was a big challenge for me, because ever since I was a little girl, I had believed in the fairy tale where Prince Charming sweeps the princess off her feet. Now I had to learn how to take care of myself, and to love me for who *I Am* - with all my strengths and weaknesses.

As a single woman, I remember many nights sitting alone feeling lonely. Knowing that it would not help to feel lonely, I would try to motivate myself to change. On most occasions I would fail and consequently end up feeling worse because I didn't succeed. Then one evening, which I still remember clearly, I was again sitting on my couch feeling lonely, when it occurred to me that I must have chosen to be alone at some deep seated heart level.

Awakened spiritually by this realization of what I had created through my thinking, I was able to recall many instances when I was formerly married and longed for "alone time." This recollection helped me to change my attitude. I began imagining that someone special would soon be attracted to me, so it was important to use my alone time wisely. I started meditating and doing some cherished hobbies. Soon, I no longer felt alone and desperate. I felt good about myself. I slowly began to realize that love is creation expressing *through* me *as* me.

Soon my life turned around and was filled with several wonderful men. Unfortunately, my pattern was to fall hopelessly in love, become emotionally dependent upon the relationship for feelings of worthiness, and then mysteriously these wonderful men would desert me. Each time this pattern repeated itself, I had a choice. Either I could continue to feel sorry for myself or I could deepen my trust in what I call my Spiritual Truth. Actually, most often I would waver between the two, and as I did, my Spiritual Truth would take over and I would dare to trust. I would trust that: *I Am Spirit individualized as Blenda,* and my true relationship as creation expressing itself in and through me is my first and paramount relationship. The more I trusted, the less I tried to figure things out. The spiritual peace I had gained began to guide me into right paths, right solutions. My life became easier and more enjoyable.

After several years and lots of fun, lots of heartache, and lots of growth, I met a man who was different from the other men I had dated. I met Raymond who is now my beloved husband at a New Year's Eve party. Funny, but I knew Raymond would be there and we would start dating. It was at that party that we first danced and felt the magic of our rhythm uplifting us to new heights of ecstasy.

Although in many ways a match in heaven, our relationship took many twists and turns before we settled into our final commitment. Even though I wanted lasting intimacy more than anything else, my fears of intimacy blocked me. I was scared of this man who communicated so well. He challenged me to look closely at the meaning of my thoughts and actions. I was challenged to face where I was stuck in my own thought patterns: they were comfortable but going nowhere. For example, I used to believe that the man had to provide the financial support and it was wrong for the woman to be successful. I believed the woman should lovingly inspire her partner, and in turn he would mysteriously know what she wanted.

I had to learn that it is not the man-woman roles that matter in a relationship. What matters is that both partners take responsibility for what they want, what they say, and for creating their own happiness.

Many people have asked me to write a book about my life and relationships, particularly about meeting and marrying the man of my dreams. Perhaps some day I will. For now, however, I desire to be of service helping people attract and have the tools they need to enjoy their ideal loving relationship. I assure you this can be a challenge. For me, for instance, moving into accepting a marriage commitment required a huge leap of faith. Before I could say "yes," Raymond, who was my fiancé had to sit with me for a couple hours while I cried and expressed many of my pent-up fears. As we moved through them one by one, they lost their power over me and ceased to be big monsters blocking me from saying "yes."

Soon Raymond and I entered into a glorious marriage. What I appreciate about our marriage is that neither of us like to be in emotional pain. Being in pain is the absence of feeling our love. By accessing our LOVE POWER, we share our thoughts and feelings from a place of Spiritual Empowerment (See the Ten Love Powers). Through Love Communication (see the chapter on Love Communication), we have created a way to communicate that quickly returns us to our shared intimacy. I have explained these communication processes in the book and they are essential secrets we practice to keep our passion alive.

I am honored to share my *LOVE SECRETS* with you. As long as you do the assignments, practice, and are willing to change your thoughts, you can be successful. Being willing is vital because it moves you from *trying to succeed to* **Expecting Success!!!**

I invite you to read *LOVE SECRETS: Falling in Love & Staying in Love.*

Now, please make yourself comfortable, prepare yourself for a lively adventure, and

EXPECT SUCCESS!

CHAPTER ONE

At The Heart Of The Matter

*"Everything that touches us,
me and you, takes us together
like a violin's bow, which
draws one voice out of two
separate strings."*

—Rainer Maria Rilke
Love Song

LOVE, THE GREATEST FORCE IN THE UNIVERSE!

Love is the greatest force in the universe, and you can use it! You are the master creator. Whether you are single or married, you can use your LOVE POWER to achieve your best dreams of loving and being loved. Love is Creation, and its energy expressing in you *as you,* is the real deal.

1

Are you single and want to attract your dream partner? Have you already experienced *Falling in Love* and want to continue *Staying in Love?* Do you long for a lasting relationship? Do you want to strengthen your power to love and be loved? Do you want to learn more? Interested? Should I go on?

When couples commit to saying "I DO," can they expect to live happily ever after when men and women are demanding more from their relationships than ever before?

Gone are the days when men were expected to be the breadwinners and women the stay-at-home moms. Usher in a new world of relationships – a world in which both men and women want to explore their inner selves through their relationships, share meaningful dialogue, enjoy good romance and sex, and prosper in a rich & fulfilling lasting relationship.

To achieve these new goals, new relationship tools are needed. Couples need to know more than how to do and say things the right way to please their partner. What is required today is to master the secrets of LOVE POWER that are within you awaiting your discovery. This book guides you so you can take the best advantage of this awesome, magnificent power. I want you to succeed. Are you willing to begin the discovery quest? We can begin right now by talking about what is a lasting relationship, why you might want one, and how you can achieve it.

What Is A Lasting Relationship?

What is a *lasting relationship?* It is a relationship that endures beyond time. The participants love and appreciate themselves for *Who They Are.* Individual self worth makes the love attraction possible while mutual acceptance multiplies and maintains the attraction. The spiritual source for a lasting relationship is LOVE POWER , a force that is greater than the individual self. LOVE POWER is based upon Universal Truth – the Nature and principles of Love. You *ARE* the LOVE POWER expressing itself *in* you, *as* you, and *through* you.

Throughout your day, you are in relationship. Whenever you interact with a person, place, or thing - *Bingo!* - you are in a relationship. Your actions and reactions to your relationship set off a stream of communication. The Hawaiian greeting, *Aloha*, acknowledges the beginning of communication between two spirits expressing themselves in human dialogue. *Aloha* means, *I greet and appreciate the Spirit in you.*

As part of *LOVE SECRETS, Falling in Love & Staying in Love,* you will learn how to ground your relationships by acknowledging the divine wonder of Love expressing itself in and through you as an individualized expression of God. As you learn how to check in and make friends with your Divine Spirit, you will discover the secrets of how to love *Who You Are*, and to attract your ideal partner, as well as to enrich your existing relationship. You will reap the benefits of knowing that as part of an All-Inclusive Divine Spirit, you can create an amazing experience in human form.

WOMEN – Have you ever noticed that when a group of women are gathered together, there is an above average probability they are talking about relationships? In fact, women often judge other women by how well their relationships are doing. They often ask each other, "Is there anyone new in your love life?" "How is your relationship going?" "Are you and your boy friend *serious?*" "Are you happy in your marriage?"

3

MEN – Most men experience that when they are no longer satisfying the relationship needs of their partners, their performance suffers both in the bedroom and the boardroom. Although relationships are important to men, they do not judge one another by how well their relationships are doing. Men tend to ask other men questions like, "So what's up?" "How is your project going?" "Have you been golfing or fishing lately?"

As you reflect upon your own life, I'd like you to think about what motivates you to have a relationship. What do you mean when you think the word relationship? Do you think of a relationship shared with one special person, or do you think about many relationships? What do you want from a relationship?

From many years as a relationship therapist, I know most people long for an intimate relationship in which they can be themselves, be appreciated for who they are, and grow together. They don't want their behavior to be judged as good or bad. What people want is to be able to relax, let their hair down, and be loved. They want to share their heights of ecstasy as well as their lows with someone who they can trust and who is special. Through all their ups and downs, they want their shared caring to last and their relationship to be a magnificent testimony of their love.

In today's world, couples want to explore their inner selves in the safety of their relationships, share sacred thoughts and feelings, enjoy romance and sex, and prosper in a mutually fulfilling life together.

Partners do not want a relationship filled with cheating, jealousy, greed, anger, fear, resentment, abandonment, and boredom. Partners want a relationship filled with trust, understanding, caring, support, romance, excitement and enthusiasm. This makes them happy, and they want this happiness to last forever.

If you want a relationship in which you are loved for who you are, share a true friendship that will last forever; then you want a *lasting relationship.*

It is important that you know how to attract and keep your special relationship. *LOVE SECRETS, Falling in Love & Staying in Love* accomplishes this goal by revealing essential relationship secrets rooted in spiritual principles. You can think of it as your Relationship Guide Book. It is that empowering! What assures the secrets working for you is your commitment to success.

Ultimately success is up to you. The ball is in your court. It is your choice! Assuming you chose to make a commitment to use the relationship secrets, you are ready to take your first step:

Say, *"Yes, I commit to being an enthusiastic student. I make time for my relationships. I promise to give the exercises my full attention. I commit to doing whatever it takes to let Love Power work for me and my relationship dreams to come true!"*

Do I Want A Lasting Relationship?

How long is a lasting relationship?

A *lasting relationship* is forever, and forever is longer than anyone can imagine.

Sometimes, after listening to a song, you discover yourself humming the tune. The melody is alive and active in you. It has become a part of you – your Truth.

Hemingway said, "Truth is stranger than fiction." Each person's reality is as unique as every snowflake and it is possible to experience a *lasting relationship* with someone special forever. The Truth of your Love will continue inspiring you long after the physical body no longer exists.

What creates a lasting relationship?

Ultimately it is your choice whether or not you have a *lasting relationship*. To understand what I mean, go back to the music analogy. What makes you choose a particular piece of music? If you had to choose between listening to classical music or heavy rock, which would you choose? What kind of music would inspire your passion? Which type of music would resonate with you? When you resonate with an experience and it awakens your passion, you have intuitively selected an experience that will last and become part of your Love Power.

Your passion is your Spiritual Being expressing your love.

You will know that you are passionate because you will be filled with enthusiasm and boundless energy. When you are passionate about what you are doing, you are in alignment with the Spiritual Being, the Spiritual Allness of *Who You Are.*

It is your Spiritual Allness, your melody, your meaning that lives forever.

I once asked a friend if she could recall a passionate experience. After thinking for a minute, she replied, "Yes, I can. Long ago, my daughter gave me a flower that she said she had picked especially for me, her Mother, whom she loves." My friend had saved this moment of passion in her memory.

When a special moment becomes part of your larger *Spiritual Allness, your Spiritual Being*, it becomes part of your eternal warehouse of memories available to you.

What about Death?

I believe that *lasting relationships* remain intact, even after death. As William Shatner said on his TV show "Is there life after life? Maybe there is!"

Personally, I believe life is eternal and spiritually we never die. We return to Creation. Spirit is eternal while the physical body passes away.

We are Spirit Beings having a human experience, and not humans having a Spiritual experience.

We know we are Spirit Beings through our intuition. Intuition is experienced uniquely for each person.

I recall vividly an intuitive spiritual experience. A year before getting married I had an encounter with my deceased mother. My mother had always wanted me to marry someone capable of loving me. Twice before our wedding, and once at our wedding reception, people called me by my mother's name which is Wendy. On these occasions, I experienced a warm glow of satisfaction as I intuitively knew my mother was sending me a message expressing her approval. Her visits gifted me with an intuitive knowledge that I was in good spiritual stead and marrying the right man.

Many people have confided in me about loved ones who have died and whose spirits continue to communicate with them, guide them, and love them. Perhaps you are one of these people.

How Do I Get One?

How to Attract a Lasting Relationship

There are three basic principles for achieving *lasting relationships.*

1. The source to empower your love is LOVE POWER - a power of Truth greater than yourself.

2. *Lasting Relationships* are aligned with your essence – you as a unique Spirit.

3. Your Spirit attracts compatibility. It is an energized magnet attracting only that with which it resonates.

Please Be Aware: These three principles will work for you to the degree that you are aware that you are Spirit and aligned with your spiritual essence. If you are not sufficiently aware and aligned with your spiritual essence, you will go through many relationships until you finally do get in alignment. You will know when you are successful because your life purpose will be clear, and you will attract a loving, *lasting relationship.* Your soul mate will be someone like you, someone with whom you resonate, someone on the same spiritual path.

What if I already have a good relationship?

The more we learn, the more we grow. A good relationship is one in which both partners are growing.

In my past, I was married to a good man. We ran a large singles club, and we were the model couple. Although our relationship was good, we struggled too hard to make it work. We didn't know how to fully trust the power of Truth greater than ourselves, or how to live in spiritual alignment with our greater purpose. Consequently, it was only a matter of time until our marriage fell apart. Disappointed, I vowed to do whatever it took to create a *lasting relationship*. For more than twenty years, I dedicated myself to this goal. Now I have achieved it. That is why I am excited to share with you what I have learned. My greatest gift is for you to fully love and be loved.

What makes this book different from other self-help books on relationships?

LOVE SECRETS, Falling in Love & Staying in Love is different than other relationship books because:

1. Its Ten Love Powers move you beyond role patterns to discover your Love Power and access your inner Truth. You design your relationships from the inside-out.

2. It recognizes that you are a Spiritual Being and can create an amazing experience in human form.

3. Old destructive beliefs that sabotage relationships are replaced by positive affirmations and *New Thoughts*. There is an inner restructuring of your thoughts – your core beliefs. *

4. Its communication techniques show you the way to move beyond difficult challenges, strengthen your relationship, and enhance your intimacy.

LOVE SECRETS, Falling in Love & Staying in Love is a relationship guide book through which you discover the relationship tools you need to build and maintain a healthy, loving relationship. These handy tools will empower you to do the right things to love and be loved by your partner.

*As you adjust your core beliefs to be in alignment with your Life Purpose, the more effective they are in serving you as intuitive guides. As Dr. Ernest Holmes said in his book entitled *This Thing Called You*, "Your whole aim is to bring your mind to a place where it unconsciously accepts the good it desires."

How do New Thoughts Work?

To show how we have changed, I am going to share some old beliefs. These old beliefs are illustrated in my parent's marriage bible, dated 1936, in *The Art of Married Life*. You will find it at the end of Chapter One. As you read it, check out what people in the 1930's believed would be the art of making a successful marriage. When you are finished, go to the next page and compare what you just read with the art of making a successful marriage as described in 2017. Do you agree that the changes are profound?

Comparing the *The Art of Married Life from 1936* to 2017, you will observe there are dramatic changes in the way we think and perceive marriage. For example, the roles that husband and wife play are far less important than they were fifty years ago. Today women are valued for who they are whether they are housewives, stay-at-home mothers, or career women. Men are also valued for who they are, whether or not they are the breadwinners or taking care of the home-front. Men are looking to women to express what they want in a way they can understand and relate to. Men want to be able to express their feelings, even cry, and still be seen as powerful. Both partners want more from their relationships: more meaningful conversations and sharing, more romance and fulfilling sex, more excitement and more exploring of their inner selves and their divine purpose.

Today's successful marriage is an intimate partnership that promotes mutual caring, freedom, and growth!

"The Art of Married Life"

Year: 1936. The chief requirement is simple enough. It is only: Put your wife, or husband, before yourself in your thoughts and choices. To the wife, this lesson is generally emphatically spoken by the circumstances into which marriage brings her. It gives her, as her chief business, the making of a home for her husband, and afterwards for her children. The event of her day is his return from work. Her work is to make him comfortable and happy.

It is when some sense of these things breaks upon the woman, in the early months of her married life that she stands face to face — as probably never before — with her destiny. And what destiny offers her is service. Bravely accepted, it will temper the whole life to celestial sweetness.

When he comes home he wants rest. He feels himself in a measure off duty. And here he gets the full comfort of a good wife, and the home that a good wife makes. He is taken in and rested and shielded from annoyance, and encompassed by a hundred gentle ministries. His body and soul find refreshment, and he is sent out a new man for the morrow's struggle. And if his wife is not allowed to give him this, she is cheated as much as he is.

"The Art of Married Life – 2017"

The chief requirement is to treat your partner as you yourself would like to be treated. Acknowledge the power for growth that your relationship offers as being greater than you believe you would achieve alone. Commit to the awesome magnificence of this wholeness. This means treating what your partner does as a sacred part of your inner journey for self discovery. Whatever your partner does, treat it with reverence for just like a mirror your relationship is reflecting back to you exactly what you need to know. As the trust and confidence in your love matures this mirroring effect deepens and reveals new levels of hidden vulnerability. It is this revealing of vulnerabilities that offers both the husband and wife quantum leaps for self discovery.

What skills are necessary for mastering the Art of Married Life? The skills required are the willingness to listen, to speak the truth, to be vulnerable, and to be heard and acknowledged. This means being open to giving and receiving in ways that are gentle, humble and mutually supportive. It means being guided intuitively to move beyond blame and criticism to participate in the wonders of a marriage-that-works.

Your marriage is much like a garden. Together you sow new seeds. In the winter when there are difficult times, the love you share carries you through the season. When spring bursts forth, you enjoy the rewards of the seeds you have sown together as husband and wife.

By Blenda R. Pilon, May 27, 2017

As you read and do the exercises in *LOVE SECRETS, Falling in Love & Staying in Love* you will master how to use *New Thoughts* to form *New Habits*. You will gain control over your outer circumstances. Your life will transform from a struggle to a magnificent experience. Using your *New Thoughts* you will design a belief system and create habits that naturally attract what you desire. Once you get the hang of it, you will see how easy and how much fun it is! It's much like going on an enjoyable thought diet. You will discover that the more consciously you choose your thoughts, the more knowledge and control you have over what happens to you. You will move your life out of automatic drive and put it into a drive that is consciously your choice. No longer will you choose to make excuses about why you can't do what you want. Instead you will be making positive choices about what you want. You will be on your way to having your fondest relationship dreams come true. Thus, the success formula:

Taking responsibility = Choosing my circumstances

Do you want to fulfill your relationship dreams?

If you answered *Yes*, it is time to treat yourself to having some fun as you start on the creation of your *New Thought* diet.

*"Think not you can direst the
course of love, for love, if it
finds you worthy, directs your course."*

—**The Prophet,** Kahil Gibran

CHAPTER TWO

Asking for What You Want

"Why does asking for what you want feel so uncomfortable?
The answer to this question is critically important to understand,
especially for women. As crazy as it might seem, complaining, arguing
and even getting downright nasty actually feels safer to most of us
than simply and directly making a request."
—Terrence Real, *The New Rules of Marriage*

THE CHALLENGE

Have you ever had the experience that you thought you knew what you wanted and when you did get it you discovered that what you got was not fulfilling? I know this happens to many people who look forward to getting married, and then some time later they discover they are not fulfilled. What they believed would happen when they got married fell apart. They mistakenly believed that when they were married they would live happily ever after with continued romance and companionship not having to do anything to maintain their relationship.

To create a marriage that works - in which we get what we want and can maintain our intimacy, we need knowledge. We need to know prior to getting married what we truly want and any blockages we may have for success. For these answers, we need to explore our own subconscious minds. Hidden in our subconscious are the answers we have been waiting to discover. To bring them out of hiding so they can be revealed by our conscious awareness, I have an exercise using four stem sentences. Stem sentences are sentences with no ending which need to be completed.

Although you can do these exercises by yourself, if possible I recommend working with a partner. You will say the stem sentence out loud and complete it. Repeat saying the sentence over and over again until you feel like you have exhausted your supply of responses. If you can't think of how to end the sentence say the word "blank" and repeat the sentence.

It is very important to repeat the stem sentences as rapidly as you can so you don't have time to *think* your answers. This way you will bypass your rational thinking and the buried thoughts in you subconscious can freely come forth into conscious awareness.

For an example of how this works, I share what happened with a client. Jim was lonely and wanted to create an intimate relationship. Using the stem sentences, Jim learned that hidden in his subconscious were feelings of guilt associated with making a final break with his wife from whom he'd been separated fifteen years. Becoming conscious of the blockage, Jim chose to free himself from his guilt feelings, get a divorce, and move forward to achieve a lasting, intimate relationship.

Now it is your turn to explore the hidden treasures buried in your subconscious mind. When you bring these beliefs into conscious awareness you can deal with them and move forward.

The four stem sentences which you repeat out load just as fast as you can are:

1. If I had a lasting relationship, I would...
2. If I had a lasting relationship, I would be willing to give...
3. If I had a lasting relationship, I would be willing to receive ...
4. What I must believe to attract my lasting relationship is...

Because the third stem sentence is difficult for many people to understand, I will give you an example of some typical response endings:

If I had a lasting relationship, I would be willing to receive....love, time off, not working so hard, passion, feeling good, being loved for who I am, appreciation, a willingness to work through concerns, flowers, romance, sex, hugs and kisses.

When you are doing this exercise with a partner, ask your partner to write down all your responses and put an * before each response that reveals heightened emotion, or that was repeated. After each question, your partner will give you constructive feedback on what you were expressing. If your partner also wants to do the stem sentences, switch roles from *expressing* to *listening* after each question.

Use the next four pages to:

- Develop your relationship goals.
- Discover any blocks you may have.
- Know your new findings came from within you.

When you are finished, pat yourself on the back. Congratulate yourself! Identifying your goals and blockages is usually more than half the solution to moving forward.

For your convenience and for keeping the pages of your book clean, please download a copy of the *Stem Sentence Exercises* at www.marriage-works.ca and go to the *Love Secrets* download.

Stem Sentence # 1

If I had a lasting relationship, I would

Write Your Responses:

_____

_____

_____

_____

_____

_____

_____

_____

_____

_____

_____

_____

_____

Notes: Put an (*) before each response that shows heightened emotion or that was repeated. Do not criticize you partner for his/her responses. Use another blank page if there are more responses.

Stem Sentence # 2

If I had a lasting relationship, I would be willing to give

Write Your Responses:

_____

_____

_____

_____

_____

_____

_____

_____

_____

_____

_____

_____

_____

Notes: Put an (*) before each response that shows heightened emotion or that was repeated. Do not criticize you partner for his/her responses. Use another blank page if there are more responses.

Stem Sentence # 3

If I had a lasting relationship, I would be willing to receive

Write Your Responses:

_____

_____

_____

_____

_____

_____

_____

_____

_____

_____

_____

_____

_____

_____

Notes: Put an (*) before each response that shows heightened emotion or that was repeated. Do not criticize you partner for his/ her responses. Use another blank page if there are more responses.

Stem Sentence # 4

What I must believe to attract my lasting relationship is

Write Your Responses:

_____

_____

_____

_____

_____

_____

_____

_____

_____

_____

_____

_____

_____

Notes: Put an (*) before each response that shows heightened emotion or that was repeated. Do not criticize you partner for his/her responses. Use another blank page if there are more responses.

From What You Have Learned Complete the Following:

My goals for a lasting relationship are:

_____

_____

_____

_____

_____

_____

_____

_____

My barriers to achieving a lasting relationship are:

_____

_____

_____

_____

_____

_____

_____

_____

Ordering What You Want

*"Asking the Universe for what you want is
your opportunity to get clear what you want.
As you get clear in your mind, you have asked."*
—Rhonda Byrne, The Secret

Thoughts become reality. The universe will deliver exactly what you ask for and believe. Ask for a penny and you will get a penny. Ask for a dollar and you will get a dollar. Ask for a million dollars, believe and live like you are receiving the money, and you will get it!

Just as the rules (Laws) for the universe are true for financial prosperity, so they are true for attracting and keeping your Ideal Relationship. To set the Universal Laws into action, ask and believe in your request. I know a single lady who wrote down a hundred attributes she wanted in her ideal partner. Much to her delight, she met a man who possessed all hundred attributes.

Here is what you can do to set the Universal Laws of Relationship Attraction in action.

First, get some lined paper and at the top write: WHAT I WANT IN MY PARTNER. List as many attributes as you want. Remember, the only limits are those you choose to make.

When you are finished, on another sheet of lined paper write: WHAT I OFFER MY PARNTER. List attributes you have to offer to your partner. Remember, the only limits are the ones your make.

Now for the fun part! When you are finished, compare the attributes you want in your partner with the attributes you are offering your partner. How many of your attributes are compatible?

An example of how crucial it is to be compatible in your lists is illustrated by a client who for his anonymity I am calling Richard. Richard is a handsome, charming banker. After writing his two lists, he compared them. In most ways they were compatible. In one way, however, they were not. Richard wanted a woman who would be faithful and devoted to him. In his own life, however, Richard would be dating one woman while he had a second woman lurking in the background just in case the first woman did not work out. Upon recognizing the discrepancy, Richard decided that when he met a woman he liked that he would be faithful to her, and her only. Two weeks later on an international flight he met a woman who took his fancy. A month later they were engaged and within the year married. After ten plus years of marriage, they continue to be "honeymooners in love."

With lists completed, you are ready to go to *Phase Three* where you keep the two lists in mind. As you meet potential partners, check your lists. Notice who you are attracting. Adjust your thoughts according to what happens. Empower your lists by believing in them and becoming the equivalent of that for which you are asking – often referred to as becoming the *living embodiment* of what you are desiring. Be mindful of your progress in attracting what you want. If someone does not work out, release him or her: Make room for the right partner. Make a game out of your journey. Joy and enthusiasm goes a long way in helping the Universe deliver your ideal mate.

Making these lists is fun and effective. If single, it invokes the Law of Attraction for your Ideal partner. If married, it keeps your marriage alive with the attributes you most desire in your partner.

Attracting Your Lasting Relationship

The story of Susan illustrates how you can attract a loving, lasting relationship. Although designed for single people, if married you can use the same process to revive and uplift your marriage.

Step 1: Clearly Ask For What You Want

Susan had a history of falling in love. Unfortunately in a matter of months after falling in love, her partner would start belittling and abusing her — sometimes emotionally, sometimes by drinking excessively and swearing at her, and sometimes by forcefully convincing Susan to do things she did not want to do. When Susan became of aware of the pattern she had created, she decided to do whatever it took to make a change.

The first thing Susan knew she had to do was to clearly ask for what she wanted in a partner. After the abuse she had suffered, Susan knew what was most important for her. Susan clearly asked for a partner who was kind and who would treat her with respect. She wanted her partner to have self confidence so he would not need to abuse and bully her to convince himself he was important.

Susan said, "As long as I have a partner who loves and respects me, the rest is icing on the cake. For example: I enjoy playing tennis, but if he doesn't play tennis that is okay. We can work out the details. I will make a list of the attributes I want and the most important is that he is capable of loving and respecting me."

Step 2: Do Not Need s Partner

In the past Susan felt she was not complete unless she had a man in her life. Although she was highly attractive, this was not enough.

The men she attracted felt her neediness. Susan got to experience first hand *"the more you need, the less you receive."* When you need something a lot you create resistance that pushes the very thing you desire away from you. In Susan's case, the more she wanted a relationship, the more she pushed it away.

In order to stop her obsessive beliefs that she needed someone, Susan made a commitment to stop criticizing herself and to end the belief that she wasn't good enough for a relationship. Instead, Susan started valuing her attributes.

Susan loved to go dancing. In the past she would always be looking for a partner. Susan's tendency was to go to dances when she wasn't feeling good about herself in hopes of meeting someone who would show interest in her and make her feel desirable. Changing to a new belief that she actually is worthwhile and desirable, Susan decided instead to go dances when she was feeling good about herself and simply wanted to have some fun.

Step 3: Appreciate Yourself

When Susan was feeling hurt, she felt unattractive. Feeling a lack of worthiness, Susan created it. When Susan realized that she was creating her own lack of self worth by entertaining unworthy thoughts, she decided to make a change. Susan decided to think about all the reasons she liked herself and how she would make the man of her dreams a good wife. As Susan made a list of her good qualities, she began to value her intelligence, musical talent, deep sincerity, compassion and sense of humor. The more Susan focused on her good qualities, the more attractive she became. Instead of coming from a place of desperation and lack, she began coming from a place of self-confidence and joy. The more Susan practiced this change, the more she attracted good experiences into her life. At last she got it! Susan realized her thoughts were a magnet attracting to her what she believed. She began having faith she would attract her perfect complement. Rather than allowing herself to be lonely and hurt, Susan made a commitment to be happy, kind and attractive.

Step 4: Visualize Your Complementary Partner

Susan began visualizing the man who would align with her good qualities and for whom she would be a good complement. To help her get clarity about what she wanted and had to offer, Susan wrote ads. She decided that it really didn't matter if she posted the ads or not, because the Universe would hear them and respond by delivering to her *clear and sincere* replies.

After writing her ad, Susan would visualize her ideal partner and imagine being with him. The next part was the exciting part. Susan would then observe who she was attracting. If it wasn't who Susan wanted, she would return to her vision board and make adjustments. She was enjoying her exciting adventure. Susan was confident the Law of Attraction was responding to her beliefs about herself, what she wanted, and her conviction.

Step 5: Be Kind To Yourself

During the process, there was a period of a couple months in which Susan was attracting abusive men. This was a red flag that indicated she needed to make a change. She could continue to worry and feel upset about what she was attracting, or she could search her thoughts and feelings to discover why she was attracting abusive men. Rather than criticizing herself, Susan chose to use her mistakes as guides to how she could make positive changes in her thinking.

Susan learned that the more she appreciated and respected herself, the more the men who were attracted to her treated her with respect and appreciation. By being kind to herself, Susan noticed that her negative attributes began to naturally disappear..

Then one day she was drawn to advice Louise L. Hay gave for good Health. It said: *1. Stop Criticizing Yourself. 2. Stop Scaring Yourself. 3. Be Kind to Yourself.*

Step 6: Love Your Belief

At last Susan believed she was ready to receive her lasting relation-ship. She had followed all the steps and trusted the universal laws of attraction to deliver answers to her requests. Susan examined her deepest feelings. She was ready and willing to receive her partner. Self-confidence and enthusiasm gave wings to her desires. Three days later Susan met the love of her life when she tripped over a log at the beach and a handsome stranger rescued her.

*Your happiness is as
important to me as
it is to you.*

—Rev. Raymond J. Pilon

CHAPTER THREE

Six Week Action Program

*"The beginning of a habit is like an invisible thread, but
every time we repeat the act we strengthen the strand, add to it
another filament, until it becomes a great cable and binds us
irrevocably, thought and action."*
—Orison Swett Marden

Working The Plan

Off with the Old! On with the New!

In many respects we are much like spiders. That part of us
which is not consciously aware builds a strong, delicate web. Before
we recognize what is happening, we are caught up in our own home-
spun web. Our life is no longer one of conscious creation – our life
is run by habits of which we are not even aware. If for some reason
this web is severed and we are awakened into conscious awareness,
we come face to face with the ultimate dilemma that is best described
by the following example:

Imagine you are a spider and hanging from your web by a mere thread. Below you twenty feet is the ground. Beneath your web, walking on the ground, is the soul mate you have dreamt about all your life. Perhaps for you, your soul mate is a pretty princess or a handsome knight. Your heart urges you to break loose of your web and pursue your dream. Imagine that lying beside you is your sword of passion. As you grab your sword and raise it to slay the binding threads of your web, you catch a glimpse of the long twenty foot drop to the ground and your potential for hurt.

Now you are faced with your ultimate dilemma. Imagine you are hanging by this one silken thread. The choice is yours. Will you cut the thread severing the web and follow your dreams, or will you climb back into the safety of your web?

What is your decision?

Why are habits important? What is their role in your life?

Most of our life is a series of habits. First we learn repetitive behaviours, and before long they become automatic. Our originating thought that created the habit gets buried in our subconscious mind. The more often we repeat the habit, the greater the influence the habit exerts in our lives.

To illustrate what I am talking about, imagine I gave you a new car and said, "This car is a gift from me to you, and it is unique. To go faster, you push up (*not down*) on the accelerator."

Now imagine you accept the gift and decide to try it out. At first you feel awkward pushing up on the accelerator to go faster; however, when you make the choice to learn the new habit, your *new conscious choice* coaches you until the new habit becomes automatic and is successfully stored in your subconscious mind.

If you do not have the relationship you desire, it is because there are old destructive beliefs buried in your subconscious mind and directing your life in ways that no longer serve you. Intuitively you know that to change, you need to make a commitment. You need to commit to an action plan for change that works. It is for this reason I have designed a six week action plan that will replace your old destructive beliefs with new thoughts and beliefs over the six week period. These new beliefs will empower you to attract, build, and enjoy a fulfilling relationship beyond your wildest dreams.

Soundly tested, these *new habits* work.

I believe that the day you start your six week action plan is the day you begin to be successful. So, put your heart into your exercises. I recommend that you make your exercises the most important thing you do for the next six weeks.

As you do the exercises, there may be times when the going seems tough and you feel like nothing is working. You may say to yourself, "Should I give up?" Well, please don't give up. These are the precise times you are making a major breakthrough and need to recommit to your plan. You can do this by simply saying to yourself, "Yes, I believe in this plan."

What I ask on your part is to have faith! Believe in your new habits. As you work with them, they will work for you. You will attract and keep that ideal relationship you have always desired.

Love is the greatest force in the Universe.
Love works for you as you work with It.

Preparing For Your Exercises

"There are no limitations to the mind except those we acknowledge."
—Napoleon Hill, *Think and Grow Rich*

Here's What You Do

ON YOUR CALENDAR: Choose a day on which to begin. Take out your calendar and mark that day as *Day Number One.* Next number each day until you reach the end of six weeks. On the forty second day, which is the final day, write the word CELEBRATION!

CHOOSING TO TAKE RESPONSIBILITY: Choosing to take responsibility is important for being successful in completing your exercises, Do you agree?

Speak this commitment aloud, write it or do both... I believe doing both is more powerful.

"I choose to take responsibility for what happens to me. My experiences are a direct result of how I react to opportunities in my life. I monitor my thoughts and feelings. Thoughts become real.

My relationships are a mirror image of my thoughts and emotions. I create what happens to me in my relationships. There is no such thing as a bad thing happening to me. *Bad* is only a way that I have chosen to think and feel. From this moment forward, I choose to release myself from all judgment that things are *bad, inadequate,* or *wrong.* Everything that happens to me is MY CHOICE. It is not my mistakes that matter, but how I handle them. My mistakes are building blocks for my growth and success.

My repeated thoughts and feelings form my habits.

I trust the new habits I am forming to guide me."

If writing out your commitment to taking responsibility, please sign it!

RECORD YOUR NEW HABITS BY FILLING IN YOU CHARTS:
At the end of this chapter are six charts – a chart for each week of your program. On the far left corner you will see the exercises listed. They are described on the next three pages. As you complete each exercise, put a check mark to indicate your successful accomplishment. The exercises are described in the next couple of pages.

Your Daily Action Exercises

Exercise One: Play Achieving Intimacy

This is an audio recording. It's purpose is to assist you in restructuring your thoughts to form new habit patterns. These new habits automatically become part of who you are – you as a Spiritual Being. Think of them as your silent partner guiding you in making desirable decisions.

To download the audio version of the self-talk tape called *Your Key To ACHIEVING INTIMACY,* go to this link: www.marriage-works.ca and go to the *Love Secrets* download.

For best results, play the audio recording for ten or more minutes a day and repeat the affirmations out loud with enthusiasm. I believe most people have better results when standing up and repeating them.

Exercise Two: Read One Love Power Each Day

The *Ten Love Powers* are described under the title: Ten Love Powers *for Falling and Staying in Love.* When you read a Love Power each day, you will complete reading each Love Power four times. Keep track of which *Love Power* you are reading in the boxes provided on the charts. The best time to read your daily *Love Power* is when you are fully relaxed (usually in the morning or evening).

Exercise Three: Meditate

Relax, make yourself comfortable, and meditate for fifteen minutes on what the *Love Power* means for you. Allow your mind to wander. Become the observer of your own thoughts and the tendencies they are revealing. Remember:

> *"Whatever the mind of man can*
> *conceive and believe it will achieve."*
> —Napoleon Hill, Think and Grow Rich

Exercise Four: Make Your Daily Journal Entry

Following your meditation, write in your relationship journal. Your daily journal entries can range from one paragraph to several pages. In your journal, describe:

1. An experience where you used the *Love Power*; or, how you imagine yourself using your *Love Power*.
2. Any beliefs you have regarding the *Love Power* that might influence your decision making and/or experiences.

Exercise Five: Believe Your Love Power

> *Believing your Love Power is like the*
> *WOW POWER of a match lighting a fire.*

When you believe your *Love Power* you are empowering it to become your coach in the decisions you make. Believing your *Love Power* is like a match lighting a fire. Your passion ignites your thought and *poof!...habits* are quickly formed and begin working for you.

Exercise Six: Treat Yourself

When you give from a full cup, you give joy and abundance. When you give from an empty cup, you give resentment and scarcity. To attract what you want, it is important to give from a full cup. "So how do you get a full cup?" One good way is to treat yourself to something that brings you pleasure every single day.

Some things that could bring you pleasure:

✓ reaching out and tell someone you care about them

✓ enjoying an ice cream cone

✓ asking for what your heart wants.

What else can you think of that makes you feel good? Whatever makes you feel good, do it!!!

Make a journal entry of what you did to feel good. When you are finished, check off the *Treated Myself* box on your chart.

What to do when you are blocked: As you make journal entries, check the appropriate box in your chart. If you are blocked, leave it blank and move on. You can always come back and fill it in later. This gives you time to discover what is causing the blockage. You may discover the cause as you work through your program, or you may want to reach out for professional coaching. Some important thoughts may be hiding in your subconscious. When you do discover what the thoughts are, you have the option of changing them.

Now on to describing each of the *Ten Love Powers* followed by examples from my workshops and clients of how it works. Why do I want to follow up with real life examples?

I believe it is helpful to have an example to follow. Through the examples I give you in the following pages, you will learn how people have used the *Ten Love Powers* to make changes in their lives. Notice how the participants often replace beliefs that don't work with *new thoughts* that do. In a second example, Tony's new thought that he and his partner would be better served by his coming from feelings of inner peace, replaces his belief that being critical of his partner will get him respect. As Tony achieves inner peace, he is able to reach out to his partner with love, compassion and understanding. Feeling understood, Tony's partner starts treating him with greater respect.

To ensure that writing in you relationship journal is an exciting adventure, please identify the old beliefs you are discarding as you choose new core thoughts. Remember, as you build your new foundation of thoughts and beliefs, they will guide you in the achievement of your relationship goals. After the *Ten Love Powers*, you will move onto the Exercise Charts.

Ten Love Powers

Falling and Staying in Love

We are living in a fast changing world. Fortunately you have some new *Love Powers* that, when practised, form habits. These habits empower you to create a lasting relationship – a relationship in which both partners enjoy *Staying in Love*.

These Love Powers are new because they go beyond telling you to do X, Y and Z to please your partner. They are different because they enable you to truly love yourself. When you interact with your partner you can come from a place of confidence and self worth.

If you can't truly love yourself, how can you expect to genuinely love your partner? At some level you will be using your partner as a way to affirm your own worth. On the other hand, when you truly love yourself, you will be able to give with no hidden agenda for receiving. When you give to your partner, it will be with pleasure – pleasure because you are so filled with love, you have plenty to share. You will not be coming from a place of neediness. You can treat your partner with the same respect and love as you would like for yourself.

To better understand what I am talking about, imagine you are in a room at a party and a couple is smiling and happy. Instinctively you know they are enjoying loving each other. Their smiles and happiness radiate a glowing atmosphere around them that is inviting and speaks loudly of their success in *Staying in Love*.

Although knowing how to please your partner, how to listen to your partner, how to make your partner feel acknowledged is important for *Staying in Love*, this is not enough. When you make a mistake in any of these very important areas, you will quickly revert back to square one: You will have fallen out of *Staying in Love*. These Love Powers are your safety net. Using them, you can make changes in your relationship while you continue to enjoy *Staying in Love*.

The reason these Love Powers are so valuable is because, when practised, they will form new habits – new automatic ways of thinking. The Love Powers empower you to be able to use your Love Power in a way that you can give love freely, without reservation. As with anything that you give freely, what you give freely returns multiplied. This a natural law of the Universe, the same as a law that makes electricity produce light. Although you can not see electricity, what it produces is real, true and powerful.

These TEN LOVE POWERS activate the invisible Love Powers that are part of a larger Universal Love Force. By using them you can enjoy *Staying in Love* forever!!!

Now, I invite you to take the next step.

Please relax and take your time. Discover for yourself the unique power of these TEN LOVE POWERS.

YOUR TEN LOVE POWERS
Including Examples of How Each Love Power Works

1. I Am Source

ALL I NEED TO STAY IN LOVE IS WITHIN ME NOW

Love is the greatest force in the Universe. Because Love is an energy of which I am a part, it follows that I Am Love Energy and "I AM the Source." I am the source and creator of everything that happens to me. Being a part of Love Energy, I have access to it. I have the capacity to love *Who I Am* and create a relationship in which I enjoy *Staying in Love.*

My fulfillment is to be able to love my partner with all my heart and in return to be loved exactly as I Am. This success is my happiness (not money or things outside of me). It is the Love Power of knowing *I AM SOURCE* that gives me courage and empowers me to deepen and enrich my relationships.

To affirm I AM Source, practice saying:

"I AM the Source of what happens to me.
I create my ideal relationship."

40

Example of Number One Love Power (How it works!)

Susan was single and overweight. She wanted to lose weight. She kept wishing she was thin. The more she wished, the more she felt desperate, unworthy, and unhappy.

Although Susan tried many diets, she could not lose weight or attract a relationship. Focusing on the new *Love Power* that *"I AM the Source of what happens to me. I create my ideal relationship."* Susan relaxed and soon felt empowered. Instead of looking to others for her answers, she began to look inward and work on her own feelings of worthiness.

Susan confided, "Once I decided I was the source of what happens to me, I started wanting to eat the right foods. I wasn't trying to lose weight any more – it happened naturally. As I moved into an acceptance of my worthiness, pounds started melting off me."

Susan recognized what Mahara Brenna said in the *Common Ground Magazine,* "There's nothing inside you can't handle because it is yours."

2. I Detach From Outcomes And Check In With My Inner Peace

Instead of constantly trying to please my partner and going into sacrifice, I detach from outcomes of what I believe I must do. I replace having to achieve outcomes with checking in with my inner peace. When something is wrong in my relationship and it is causing a pain in my heart or gut, I stand back emotionally from what I am doing and focus my attention into a calm, peaceful feeling. This automatically connects me with my Love Power. Relaxed, I listen to the messages that my Love Power provides me. I know intuitively these messages are my inner guides. I listen to and interact with my inner guides to enhance my understanding of important issues such as: *Who I Am, How I can Best Express My Love to My Partner, and What do I Require to Further My (and Our) Growth.*

I know that my inner peace is infinite Love Power. It connects me to the source of my Truth - my *LOVE POWER.* I no longer have to figure out the details of how to get what I want. Being at peace is the key that enables me to unlock and tap into this Truth."

To affirm that I detach from outcomes and check in with my inner peace, I practice saying:

"I AM Peace. I AM Infinite Love Power."

Example of Number Two Love Power (How it works!)

"The journey of spirituality is one of surrender. We must teach intuitive development. Developing the interior is what matters because self esteem is the key."
—Caroline Myss

Tony and his wife were constantly arguing. Tony liked to believe he was in charge of his life and could run his married life as if he were the captain of his ship. One day while sitting at the breakfast table, his wife told him, "You look awful unshaven; you haven't picked up your clothes, and I'm really upset that you arrived home late from work with no explanation of why you were late."

"Normally," Tony confessed, "I would be very upset with such comments because if I accepted them I would no longer be captain of my ship. I would lose my control position. I was unable to detach from wanting an outcome of being the partner in our relationship who was the leader and in control. Upset and angry that living a life where I was in control was being threatened, I would raise my voice and say to my wife in harsh tones, 'Constantly checking up on what I do proves you don't trust me. What is the matter with you that you can't trust me?'"

Tony leaned forward in his chair as if to confide in me a deep dark secret and said, "Finally this one time, I was so sick and tired of bullying my wife and seeing her hurt expression when I raised my voice that I decided to forget bullying her and wanting control..

I decided to make a new choice and to *walk in my wife's shoes*, understand where she was coming from, and respond to her from a place of inner peace."

Tony went on exuberantly to share, "What happened next was incredible. My wife soon stopped blaming me for her unhappiness and instead began asking me what she could do to make me more comfortable when I arrived home from work.

Through this experience, I discovered that *my inner peace is my power and that "I AM PEACE. I AM INFINITE LOVE POWER.".* Armed with this new realization, I stopped trying to be captain of my ship and control through criticism and nasty little put downs. Instead, I purposefully gave my wife love and understanding. In return, I have received more respect and caring than I ever imagined possible."

3. I Choose Harmony And Growth

Being in harmony with your partner is your assurance that you that you are *Staying in The Love*. Relationship harmony is like floating downstream and is effortless. In contrast, going upstream requires effort and is an indication that you are not in alignment with either yourself, or with your partner. You can still grow, but it will be at the expense of pain and the anxiety that results from trying. To make *Staying in Love* easy, choose Harmony and Growth.

To affirm your choice of harmony and growth, practice saying:

"I choose thoughts of harmony and growth!"

Example of Number Three Love Power (How it works!)

"Let us be silent that we may hear the whispers of God."
—Ralph Waldo Emerson

In a coaching session, Julia told me, "My husband, Derrick, was always giving me suggestions. His suggestions included everything from the way I cook bacon to the way I feed the baby. Soon his suggestions really upset me, and I ended up either going completely silent or leaving the room. I felt as if I was constantly being nagged and criticized. In an effort to be ready to dodge Derrick's critical remarks, I walked on eggshells.. My mind was always *on* alert. It was hard for me to be happy in this caustic atmosphere."

Finally the realization came to me that what happens to me in our relationships can be easy or difficult depending on how I think and react. I decided to make a change. Instead of allowing my thoughts to focus on how mean Derrick was being to me, I decided to take a deep breath and move into a place of inner peace and love power. When I reached this place of peace, I discovered I was able to refocus my thoughts and thank Derrick for his suggestions. Sometimes I was so rooted in my peace and love power that in a gentle way I was able to let Derrick know how I felt. For example, sometimes I would ask Derrick to first give me a compliment before making suggestions and that would make it feel like he cared about me. Then sometimes I would simply agree with Derrick that he had a good point of view. After Derrick felt acknowledged, I would add my opinion. By first acknowledging the importance of Derrick's suggestion, he was able to appreciate my way of thinking."

"That is very insightful," I complimented Julia.

Julia replied, "Well, you know, I am rewarded whenever I *choose thoughts of harmony.* As I acknowledge my husband's suggestions, it puts us in a flow of harmony. It is like we are in a rowboat floating downstream rather than struggling to paddle upstream against the current. When we flow downstream together, my creative energy is freed up. I am happy. Working together, Derrick and I are growing stronger in our mutual respect and intimacy. There is a new level of honesty between us, and guess what? Our love and sharing has taking a quantum leap forward."

4. My Relationships Mirror My Thoughts

I am the only person who can create what happens to me in my relationship with my partner. I am also the only person who can create what happens to me in my other relationships. Knowing this, I accept that I, and I alone, am responsible for creating happiness in my relationships. *Staying in Love* is my choice and my creation.

Because I have volition (the power of choice), I get to choose thoughts of love or fear. With practice, it is just as easy to choose thoughts of Love as it is to choose thoughts of fear. I CHOOSE TO THINK LOVE THOUGHTS! As I think love thoughts, I observe my love lighting up my relationships with what I desire and dark shadows of fear fade into oblivion. I trust this Divine Love: It is my Truth. As I make a *MORAL COMMITMENT* to believe in *Its* power, *It* functions as an energized magnet attracting to me exactly what I need. My intimate relationship with my partner provides me with a glorious reflection of Who I Am and all that I can become.

To affirm that my relationships mirror my thoughts, I practice saying,

"My relationships are an exact mirror of my thoughts"

Example of Number Four Love Power (How it works!)

Jack said, "I used to go to singles dances hoping to meet "Mrs. Right." I put so much pressure on myself to find my perfect mate that I became terribly anxious. After repeated rejections from women, I couldn't eat or sleep. I felt worthless. Finally, I knew I had to do something different.

Rather than trying to make a change on the outside, I decided to make a change on the inside. I wanted to demonstrate to myself that a change in thoughts would transform what was happening on the outside of my life. I wanted to know that a change in thought (cause) would make a change in my experiences (effect).

The thought I decided to change was not to attend the dances with the intention of meeting my life-long partner, but rather to attend the dances with the intention (*new thought*) of wanting to meet a friend. This *new thought* allowed me to stop being so wrapped up in my own success. When I was no longer under this pressure, I could listen to what people had to say and create friendships. I discovered I could be more real about myself. I even took the risk to reveal deep, long-standing secrets. Much to my delight, I found that the more I exposed my true self, the better I was liked.

Now I am a happy trooper. I have attracted friends, and I know that when I am ready, the right woman for me will appear. I'm having fun, and I've learned that *my relationships are an exact mirror of my thoughts.*"

5. My Mistakes Are Creative Opportunities

> *"I learned that courage was not the absence of fear,*
> *but the triumph over it."*
> —Nelson Mandela

Partners come together with their own unique thoughts and values. There are bound to be differences of opinion and different ways of handling situations. In a young relationship these differences often lead to a power struggle. In more seasoned relationships these differences often lead to arguments, resentment, abuse and stubborn defiance.

Unfortunately partners are not aware of the impact of these differences until they are suffering the consequences. It takes constant vigilance to watch your thoughts and to observe what they are creating. Sometimes it is close to impossible, because you are not conscious of your thoughts,. It is as if they are mysteriously rising out of a deep unknown source. Even though these thoughts are unconscious, they are powerful.

There are two ways you can handle unwanted thoughts (whether they are conscious or unconscious). One way is to ignore the unwanted thoughts and suffer the consequences. A second way is to acknowledge what the unwanted thoughts have created, recognize them as a mistake (wrong thought), and correct the mistake by changing your thoughts. Of course, by changing your thinking (cause) you automatically create a new outcome (effect). If you choose the second way, the unwanted thought becomes a creative opportunity for you to change your thoughts until you succeed in getting what you want.

In your relationship with your partner, it is important to be mindful of what is happening. When there is a power struggle or conflict, explore your thoughts until you discover what thoughts consciously or unconsciously have created the unwanted outcome. Instead of being upset, bless these thoughts and the opportunity they give you to make changes and correct mistakes. Think only of what you want. Remember, your mistakes are stepping stones to success.

A good way to turn mistakes into creative positive opportunities is to practice saying:

"My mistakes are creative opportunities.
They are my stepping stones to success."

Example of Number Five Love Power (How it works!)

Susan is a housewife. She complained that all she ever did was take care of the home and her three boys. What Susan wanted to do was to have a job outside the home and be creative. Susan was bored, and often tired and grouchy in the evenings.

Aware that she was grouchy and not getting what she wanted, Susan realized that she must be doing something wrong and at a gut level she knew she could make this into a creative opportunity. Instead of doing all the housework herself, Susan invited her family to make cooking and cleaning part of a family affair. Much to Susan's delight, her boys enjoyed helping her and she began to have fun teaching them what she knew. Before long, her boys insisted on doing most of the cooking. This freed up time for Susan to share more quality experiences together. The whole family felt better and Susan's grouchiness was replaced with smiles, laughter and kindness. Susan was so delighted she accepted a part time, rather than a full time job. Having corrected her mistake of trying to do everything herself, Susan was able have both her career and family dreams come true.

Through this experience Susan was able to trust that *"My mistakes are creative opportunities. They are my stepping stones to success."*

6. I Embrace Well Being

When a couple gets married, typically they decide to be emotionally available for each other in sickness and in health. This is an important reminder that in a committed relationship, partners join together to form a larger whole. Your life and your decisions are made with your partner in mind. How you are feeling and acting affects the well being and happiness of both you and your mate. You are no longer alone – you are part of a synergistic whole that is larger than you.

I believe that in our human experience everyone is working to create a better situation for themselves. It can be in one or more of three areas of well being: relationships, health, financial prosperity. As a committed partner, it is important to *EMBRACE WELL BEING* for both yourself and your partner. If either you or your partner is not well, then the dynamics of your relationship will change.

It is important for you and your partner to know and affirm that as Spiritual Beings you are Whole, Complete and Perfect. In your human experience, you can choose to make real your spiritual magnificence by practising thoughts of health and happiness in your intimate relationship. You can consciously use your thoughts to create respect, caring and passion in that relationship, in your body, and all areas of prosperity.

To *Embrace Well Being* practice saying:

"I Embrace Well Being. I am whole,
complete and perfect just the way I AM."

Example of Number Six Love Power (How it works!)

Ralph held down a responsible job as a manager. When he arrived home in the evenings he was stressed out. To unwind, Ralph would watch television, smoke, and have a couple of drinks. After a couple of years of being stressed out, his doctor warned Ralph that he had gained too much weight and suffered from high blood pressure.

Ralph recognized these warning signals. He knew enough to appreciate that a change in thoughts would make a change in his experiences and become reality. "*As within, so without,*" Ralph would repeat to himself. Ralph had a critical choice to make. He knew that he could hold onto his old thoughts and watch his blood pressure rise and his health deteriorate, or he could choose *new thoughts of well being* that would create health and happiness.

Ralph decided to practice new Well Being thoughts such as "*I Embrace Well Being. I am whole, complete and perfect just the way I AM.*" Faithfully Ralph disciplined himself and practiced these thoughts many times daily.

Before long, Ralph was experiencing more energy and was feeling better. He started swimming twice a week and woodworking on the weekends. Within two months, Ralph had shed fifteen pounds and his blood pressure was back to normal.

Choosing *new thoughts* of wellness were working for Ralph. His crowning victory came when he overheard his wife tell her mother, "Ralph is looking better than he did when we were married ten years ago." With compliments such as his wife's, Ralph became passionate about doing his exercises and expanded it to three times a week. Like whipped cream on top of his cake, his sexual intimacy with his wife reached unparalleled heights. Ralph said, "I feel like a new man!"

7. I Trust My Love Power

> "*The flow of love outward into the world is
> the creative impulse of life.*"
> —Jonathan F Pratt, *The Purpose and Love Manifesto*

Getting married is not only glorious, it is magical. When you get married and are in the honeymoon state, it seems like nothing can go wrong. Then when the magic dust settles, often differences in opinions and ways to handle things appears. That is why power struggles happen – each partner wants to be in control and to be right. Later in the relationship many challenges arise. In most committed relationships, this is normal. The benefit of having challenges is that they give you an opportunity to trust in your Love Power. True, you can't see your Love Power. Equally true, you can see the results of your Love Power when you trust and believe in it. Perhaps you can identify with a partner who asks you to do something such as to make dinner or take out the garbage, and your partner has a sharp voice that automatically makes you feel abused and resentful. Now, when this same partner is acting from LOVE POWER, he or she will ask you to do the same thing using a soothing tone and words of gratitude that let you know they appreciate your help.

So, when you trust your LOVE POWER – when you have faith in your LOVE POWER, any obstacle can be overcome.

What determines what is right for you is your LOVE POWER, and not your *everyday me* that tries to figure out solutions. Your LOVE POWER is your true guide. No relationship, person, or event is the source of your power. Your power lies in your awareness of Love - its laws and principles. This awareness forms your intuitive insights that guide you. Love Energy is present in and through everything."

Funny, I just heard a song that was put out by Steve Jobs at Apple computer that repeats over and over again, "All there is, is LOVE!!" If you hear it, remember the catchy tune.

To trust your Love Power, practice saying:

"All there is, is LOVE!! "

Example of Number Seven Love Power (How it works!)

Ashley shared with me how a challenging situation with her husband gave her greater trust in her Love Power.

Shawn was fired from his job with the forest industry. For a year he searched without success for a new job. Ashley told me, "This was a difficult time for both Shawn and me. I assumed financial responsibility. Because of Shawn's inability to find work, I had to put up with snide remarks from many of my women friends suggesting that there was something wrong with me because I was doing a man's job supporting the family financially."

Ashley continued, "Although I kept wishing that our struggle would end, instead it got worse. No one wanted to hire Shawn. Our pocketbooks were nearly empty. Just when I felt like giving up, Shawn came home elated. He was offered an opportunity to buy into a stained glass manufacturing company. He was so excited that I intuitively felt his inner passion re-surging. That was a WOW moment for me. A voice deep inside me whispered that his passion had been the missing ingredient. I believed Shawn's newly awakened passion would attract success.

I asked myself, "Can I really trust Shawn's passion to be an indicator that his true purpose is working through him? If I support Shawn's desire to buy into the stained glass company, I'll have to use my hidden reserve money. I'll have to trust my inner Love Power that we will be financially supported."

Feeling somewhat fearful, I recalled the words of President Teddy Roosevelt who said, "The only thing to fear is fear itself."

"I was so scared," confessed Ashley, "I knew fear attracts the very thing we fear. So, to override my fear, I pretended I was skydiving off a cliff and trusted that I would experience a miracle landing."

"Unfortunately my efforts in overcoming my fear failed terribly. We used up my reserves and were forced to borrow money. Now I was darn right scared and didn't know what to do, or to whom to turn. The only Truth that kept coming up for me was the trust in my Love Power was not yet strong enough."

"Believing that trust is a spiritual quality, I decided to ask my *Love Power* for help. When I did, my *Love Power* guided me to share more intimately with Shawn. So, Shawn and I talked. After much discussion, we decided to think of the stained glass business as *our* business. To make it truly our business, we opened up a joint account in a new business name, and committed to depositing $20 per week into it."

"Experiencing a deeper heart-connection with Shawn plus adding to our modest business account weekly inspired me to trust more deeply in the Power of our Love. We began daily repeating, *All there is, is LOVE!!*. Before long we had a thousand, then two thousand, then ten thousand dollars. Trusting in our *Love Power*, I became conscious of the importance of being guided by Spirit. Shawn and I became successful, in fact, successful beyond what we ever imagined possible. After this experience, Shawn and I are willing to take on any challenge we believe is worthwhile."

8. Being Truthful Sets Me Free

When you have a personal problem or you are annoyed by something your partner is doing, you have a choice. You can either keep your concern to yourself or share your concern with your partner. Although it is more intimate to share, many people choose to keep their concerns private. The potential danger of making this choice is that concerns can easily fester and grow in their emotional impact, and before long you may feel resentful or hurt. When you choose to be truthful with your partner you release this potential emotional impact. To be truthful is freeing, and yet to be truthful can be a challenge. That is why I have included the chapter on Love Communication. It shows you the way to move from anger back to love and heightened intimacy.

When you are truthful with your partner, all fear and guilt feelings that you have been hiding are automatically discharged. Being honest and truthful with your partner sets both you and your partner free. Love Energy can freely work for you.

To be truthful with your partner, practice saying:

"Sharing with my partner sets me free.
I enjoy sharing my truth."

Example of Number Eight Love Power (How it works!)

Here is a story Nelson told me: "I didn't know what to do. I felt starved. Rationally, I knew Judy loved me, but hard as I tried, I couldn't feel her love. We'd been married seven years and not once in the last four years had she made a sexual advance toward me. At night when I finally persuaded her it was time for bed, she would lie on her side of the bed like a stiff baby doll. I began to believe I was married to a woman who was half corpse. Judy was stiff, cold, and made me feel inadequate.

One day I was feeling so bad that my gut ached. I knew things had to change. I had suffered enough. All I could do was to lie on the living-room couch and confess to Judy how awful I felt, then humbly ask her for support.

Feeling my pain and love for her, Judy started crying. Judy explained to me that she had begun to think that all I wanted her for was to clean house and take care of the children. So, Judy confessed that she started faking orgasms, then faked wanting to go to bed, and finally faked being in love with me. My wife said that she did not know what caused this, but suspected that it might have started when her uncle abused her as a child. Judy promised to see a sex therapist about her suspicion.

Judy went to see a sex therapist and grew immensely from her visits. Now Judy and I check in with ourselves before we make love. If there is anything bothering us, we either express it or decide not to make love until we both feel like it. Both of us know *being truthful with one another sets us free*. We enjoy sharing our truths. As a result, you should see Judy when she's willing. She is a real tigress. To tell you the truth, I suspect she is making up for lost time. Well, lucky me!!! I am a living example of every man's dream come true!!!"

9. I Am Thankful For All I Have

"When we cultivate a consistent attitude of gratitude,
we manifest even more to be grateful for."
—Shri Ananda; film producer, Out of The Darkness, 2016

When you are concerned about your relationship and feel angry, resentful or confused, the best way to turn things around is to give thanks for all you have. Being thankful is an expression of gratitude and moves you from scarcity to abundance. It warms your heart filling you with LOVE POWER.

When you have gratitude, you are able to forgive your partner for any negative feelings or experiences you believe your partner has created. You enjoy taking responsibility for your own happiness, and you spontaneously give from a full cup. You have plenty to share, and know that to give with joy is to receive with pleasure.

To be thankful for all you have, practice saying:

"I give thanks for all I have.
I have plenty to share."

Example of Number Nine Love Power (How it works!)

This is based on a true story Nan shared with me: "I lay in the hospital recovering from a heart attack. I should have died, but didn't. Looking around the empty hospital room mirrored my empty heart, my empty life. I was all alone while my supposed boy friend was only an hour's drive away.

I know that a part of me had wanted a change for a long while. Now as if an emergency alarm bell had rung inside of me, I had created necessary quiet time to reflect upon my life patterns. Because my heart had once again been broken, I suspected my heart was begging for some tender loving care and attention. I decided to do whatever it took to fill my heart with an abundance of love.

That night my boy friend called claiming he did not want to hurt me, but his schedule wouldn't allow him to visit me the next day. With open attentive heart, I caught his intention. I took charge and told him not to bother visiting, and the only person who was capable of hurting me was me. Then I got so brave I told him I was releasing him from my life to find another better-suited partner.

Amazingly, I felt great after my declaration. I felt as if I had claimed back my life. I closed my eyes and gave thanks for all I have and the courage to take responsibility for what happens to me.

Daily I started repeating this affirmation: *"I give thanks for all I have. I have plenty to share."*

With an open heart, I moved forward. Soon a new partner was attracted to me. My new husband is kind and gentle. I believe the attraction happened because I was thankful for all I have.

10. I Choose To Become That Which I Desire To Receive

*"Be the relationship you want to have in you your life.
If you are single, you have to BE that person yourself
before you can attract the one you want."*
—Rev. Carrie Hunter, Centre for Spiritual Living,
Victoria, BC, Canada

When you become that which you desire to receive, the Law of Attraction automatically fulfills your desires.

For your partner to make desirable changes, it is important for you to become that for which you are asking. For example, if you want your partner to acknowledge your good qualities, you acknowledge your partner's good qualities. To take another example, if you want a hug then give your partner a hug. If you want your partner to show you more love and affection, you give your partner more love and affection. It is guaranteed that becoming what you desire sets the Law of Attraction in motion delivering to you what you desire. Like attracts like!

To become that which you desire to receive, practice saying:

"I choose to become that which I desire to receive."

Examples of Number Ten Love Power (How it works!)

*Because this can be a challenging LOVE POWER
to put into action, there are three examples!*

Example One – For Singles

This example is from a single's club called Singles International that I managed many years ago and although my memory is a bit hazy, I do vividly remember that what Amy wanted was a common desire of many young women who were members of Single's International.

Amy wanted to attract a wealthy man, a man who was a shining night in armour and would support her in grand style.

Intent on her goal, Amy said to me, "There are some really good men in this Single's Club and I want to attract one as my mate. What is the secret to making this happen?"

I asked Amy, "So what are you doing to make this happen?"

Amy replied, "I am wearing the latest fashions, have had my hair done by an expensive hair stylist, and flirt like crazy with the men who I desire as a mate."

"Are you having any success? What is happening?" I asked Amy.

Amy replied, "To tell you the truth, it seems like the more I try the worse it gets. The men are either polite or they are only after my body."

This prompted me to ask Amy, "If you were a wealthy man, would you feel comfortable considering someone for a life-long partner who didn't have much wealth? Would you be suspicious that such a woman wanted you for your money and not for who you are?"

Amy saw my reasoning and wondered what to do about it. She wanted a wealthy man, but she wasn't wealthy.

I explained to Amy, "To attract a wealthy man, you must believe so completely you are wealthy that you start living like a wealthy person would live. As the expression goes, *you become the living embodiment of your desire.*"

Amy replied, "That sounds nearly impossible. How would I go about doing such a thing?"

Together we made a plan. The first requirement was that Amy start giving gratitude for all she has and through this process build up her belief that she is a worthwhile woman. The next requirement was for Amy to take something she was passionate about, and in her case it was photography, and to more actively pursue her passion. The last requirement that we designed together was for Amy to volunteer giving freely of her gift when it seemed appropriate.

Implementing this plan, Amy built-up her belief that she was worthwhile. She also began to feel wealthy because she was able to give freely (without charging) for some of her photography. Now when she shared conversations with the men, she was a powerful women who had skills and was generous.

Amy said to me, "I feel much better and the the men are treating me differently. They look me in the eye, smile at me, and one man asked me to take some photos of him golfing and another man invited me to go sailing with him on his yacht. I am having so much fun I am in no rush to find that perfect wealthy man."

Well, can you guess the rest of the story? I bet you can. Yes, with the pressure off and believing she was worthwhile (this is the kissing-cousin to being financially wealthy), Amy began embodying and acting like a wealthy woman. Of course, it wasn't long before Amy attracted the love of her life – and he was wealthy! Amy and her partner got engaged, and soon after were happily married.

Now when I think of Amy and the many other women who want to attract a wealthy man, I am reminded of the country song where the words go something like this: "Do what you will do well. Love with all your heart, and do what you will do well."

Example Two

Cassandra came to me for sexual coaching and this is what she told me: "I used to feel like the main reason my boyfriend liked me was for s-e-x. Gradually my attitude affected my lovemaking. I felt bored and soon discovered my mind was frequently drifting. One night I was doing just that – I was drifting."

"Put yourself into what you are doing and really enjoy yourself," my boyfriend, Aaron, directed me.

As if awakening me from a trance, I answered Aaron, "Oh! Okay!"

Cassandra continued, "Inwardly, I was shocked. I was amazed my boyfriend could tell when I wasn't paying attention! What a fool I was. Of course he could tell!"

I said to myself, "I'll show my boyfriend, Aaron. I'll put my heart into what I am doing. 'I'll do and become that which I desire to receive."

Immediately Aaron noticed the difference. "That's great!" Aaron purred as my fingers stroked his body tenderly, "You can do that all night. It feels marvellous. What a difference!"

I mused to myself, "Yes! What a difference, and the biggest difference is my own experience. I've decided to give up being resentful and enjoy myself. It is like I lifted an invisible barrier. Suddenly I can feel the warmth and sensitivity of Aaron's skin and can feel his warmth and caring as he touches me. Love and passion vibrates through all the cells of my body. This is real love, living in the moment, and daring to do what I would like to receive - alive to all my senses. *How I am experiencing life is a reflection of how fully I am living that which I desire to receive.*"

Example Three

Chris arrived at my office angry and looking defeated.

Slouched down in his chair with head bent over, Chris confided, "I can't go on any longer like this. I don't know what to do. My wife, Anna, is abusing me mentally and it is driving me to drinking. She says I'm a lazy bum and *no good for nothing*. The last thing I want is to become is a raging alcoholic like my wife's Dad was. How can I handle this situation?"

"Chris," I said, "I understand why you are so uncomfortable and want to change what is happening. Are you willing to make some changes starting with your thinking?"

"I am ready," Chris eagerly replied.

I then coached Chris, "Number one you need to know and accept deep down that you are worthy and do not deserve to be abused. Can you do this?"

"If I think of how well I did in football, then I might be able to feel worthy. The only trouble is I am no longer playing football," said Chris.

To put Chris at ease I said to him, "You don't have to be playing football to make your memory work for you. Imagine *as if* you are still active in football, how good you are and how the other players value you. Congratulate yourself for a job well done and pat yourself on the back! Give yourself permission to feel good. When you do, let your imagination take you to other situations when you know you did well. Have gratitude for those situations - gratitude is like love and will grow your good feelings and self esteem."

"Okay, I can do this" said Chris, and then added "Then what?"

"Next is to picture yourself just the opposite of what Anna is claiming. Imagine yourself being full of energy, doing the things you like to do, helping around the house, and having friends who like you and ask for your help."

Chris decided to try this out and came back a month later. He said, "Everything is going much better and I am not so affected by what my wife is saying as she tries to abuse me mentally. I just need a little more power to completely overcome the abuse. So what can I do next?"

I recommended that Chris imagine the abuse his wife was giving him to be like little mud bombs she was throwing at him and that he could duck and dodge them thus avoiding them hitting and affecting him. Next he should stand tall and use his LOVE POWER to send his wife loving thoughts. To the thoughts he could attach words such as, "You know I love you. I am here for you if you want to talk – I will always be your friend."

After this last session it was only two weeks later that Chris arrived for another session. He began by saying, "This stuff really works. Instead of feeling like a *poor old me abused husband* I was thinking like and believing I was a *deserving, loving husband*. My wife couldn't resist the *new me* and soon started confiding in me and even having some fun with me. I believe that when she was abusing me she had been thinking of me like I was her old man. Now she has decided to mentally release her dad and instead embrace her husband, ME! From now on I'm going to become that which I desire – it is magic and really works in getting me what I want. Thank you! You deserve my appreciation and gratitude. I just wanted to come in to thank you and tell you that you have done such a good job that I won't be needing your help for awhile – probably a long while."

As you practice your Ten Love Powers, embrace the following belief:

"I choose to enjoy loving, lasting intimacy with my partner.
I have the LOVE POWER to make my desires come true!"

A Quick Reference Summary of your Ten LOVE POWERS follows on the next page.

Quick Reference:
Summary of TEN LOVE POWERS

When you make a copy of your TEN LOVE POWERS and their affirmations, you can easily practice them until they become your cherished habits.

1. I Am Source

> *"I AM the Source of what happens to me.*
> *I create my ideal relationship."*

2. I Detach From Outcomes And Check In With My Inner Peace

> *"I AM Peace. I AM Infinite Love Power."*

3. I Choose Harmony And Growth

> *"I choose thoughts of harmony and growth!"*

4. My Relationships Mirror My Thoughts

> *"My relationships are an exact mirror of my thoughts."*

5. My Mistakes Are Creative Opportunities

> *"My mistakes are creative opportunities.*
> *They are my stepping stones to success."*

6. I Embrace Well Being

> *" I Embrace Well Being. I am whole, complete*
> *and perfect just the way I AM. "*

7. I Trust My Love Power

> *" All there is, is LOVE!! "*

8. Being Truthful Sets Me Free

Sharing with my partner sets me free. I enjoy sharing my truth."

9. I Am Thankful For All I Have

"I give thanks for all I have. I have plenty to share."

10. I Choose To Become That Which I Desire To Receive

"I choose to become that which I desire to receive."

6 Week Action Program Chart

Instructions: Put a check mark as you do each exercise as shown on the sample for Day One under *Played Achieving Intimacy.* Do your best to do each exercise every day. *Keeping* your commitment to do the exercises will assure your success!

WEEK 1	Mon (1)	Tues (2)	Wed (3)	Thurs (4)	Fri (5)	Sat (6)	Sun (7)
Played *Achieving Intimacy*	✓						
Read 1 *Love Power*							
Meditated							
Made Daily Journal Entry							
Believed My *Love Power*							
Treated Myself							

WEEK 2	Mon (1)	Tues (2)	Wed (3)	Thurs (4)	Fri (5)	Sat (6)	Sun (7)
Played *Achieving Intimacy*							
Made Daily Journal Entry							
Read 1 *Love Power*							
Meditated							
Believed My *Love Power*							
Treated Myself							

WEEK 3	Mon (1)	Tues (2)	Wed (3)	Thurs (4)	Fri (5)	Sat (6)	Sun (7)
Played *Achieving Intimacy*							
Read 1 *Love Power*							
Meditated							
Made Daily Journal Entry							
Believed My *Love Power*							
Treated Myself							

WEEK 4	Mon (1)	Tues (2)	Wed (3)	Thurs (4)	Fri (5)	Sat (6)	Sun (7)
Played *Achieving Intimacy*							
Read 1 *Love Power*							
Meditated							
Made Daily Journal Entry							
Believed My *Love Power*							
Treated Myself							

WEEK 5	Mon (1)	Tues (2)	Wed (3)	Thurs (4)	Fri (5)	Sat (6)	Sun (7)
Played *Achieving Intimacy*							
Read One *New Thought*							
Meditated							
Made Daily Journal Entry							
Believed My *Love Power*							
Treated Myself							

WEEK 6	Mon (1)	Tues (2)	Wed (3)	Thurs (4)	Fri (5)	Sat (6)	Sun (7)
Played *Achieving Intimacy*							
Read 1 *Love Power*							
Meditated							
Made Daily Journal Entry							
Believed My *Love Power*							
Treated Myself							

For your convenience and for keeping the pages of your book clean, please download a copy of the *6 Week Action Program Chart* at www.marriage-works.ca and go to the *Love Secrets* downloads.

THE WARRIOR'S PRAYER

I am what I am.
In having faith in the beauty
within me, I develop trust.
In softness I have strength.
In silence I walk with the gods.

—Stuart Wilde, *Affirmations*

CHAPTER FOUR

Unmasking Myths

"Consciousness means the inner embodiment of an idea through the recognition of Truth and a direct relationship to the Divine."
—Dr. Ernest Holmes, The Science of Mind

Exploring Myths

Have you ever wondered about the expression, "You are perfect just the way you are?" I pondered the meaning for several years. Finally I came to believe it means that in this moment I AM perfect just the way I AM. Since my *I AM* is evolving, it is also true that I AM perfect at each point along my personal continuum of spiritual growth. In Truth, there is no such thing as being right or wrong, or not as good as someone else. What is true is that we are on a spiritual journey of inner growth and breaking through limiting belief patterns to a higher frequency of vibration, ease and joy in our lives.

This chapter, *Unmasking Myths,* explores relationship myths, sexual myths, and emotional barriers that frequently lay buried in the subconscious. These myths and emotional barriers act as ego resistors. They fight you in your attempt to incorporate *new thoughts* into your core beliefs. Becoming aware of these ego resistors, you can control their influence. For example, when you recognize a certain thought (belief) that is holding you back from changing, you can make the choice to delete the old belief and replace it with a *new thought,* or to stay comfortable in the repetitive behavior pattern. As long as you are aware and consciously making a choice, you are in control and will build self confidence.

Because I believe actions speak louder than words, I am going to give you an example of what I mean. Betty is a very popular woman who attracts many men. Every time Betty starts getting close to a man, an old lover named Shaun calls her long distance. Shaun confides in Betty that he could never live with her because they are so different; yet, Shaun keeps her dangling by a string. One way Shaun dangles Betty is by getting very upset when she gets involved with another man. This confuses Betty. Shaun is so charming that he continues to attract her. On the other hand, Betty despises Shaun for dangling the carrot of love and long-term relationship. Part of Betty wants Shaun while another part despises him. Sound familiar?

In the case of Shaun and Betty, it is obvious that both parties are suffering pain. Interestingly, the pain is acceptable because it enables both participants to continue to avoid intimacy. When either Betty or Shaun become aware of how the pain is serving them, they are ready to make one of three choices: 1) to share their new awareness with the other partner and encourage moving beyond their fear of intimacy, 2) to separate from the painful relationship and move on to another relationship that promises intimacy, or 3) to accept the pain as a way to avoid intimacy.

Unmasking myths and breaking through relationship barriers is a choice. Is it a choice you consciously make? As long as you are consciously making choices, your self-confidence increases and problems automatically start disappearing. The most powerful thing you can do for yourself as you learn about the relationship myths and barriers is to have fun and make conscious choices. Remember, the continued use of repetitive thoughts leads to forming habits that are stored in your subconscious. It is these thoughts that, left unchecked, run your life.

Plant a seed
Sow the soil with love
Then let seed go and grow
Into a flower just right for you.

Relationship Myths

1. MYTH: Commitment is valid only as long as my relationship is good

TRUTH: One of the most common and destructive myths is that you should stay in your relationship *only* as long as it is good. According to this myth, when you experience disappointment and/ or struggle your commitment is no longer valid. It is perfectly okay to leave the relationship and even to blame outside factors. The belief that is acted upon is: "If the relationship is not working for you, it is fine to leave – there is a *back door* for easy escape."

If you believe the myth that *commitment is valid only as long as my relationship is good*, you are setting the stage for disappointment and struggle. The myth gains power over you because you have stopped trusting in your Love Power. You will lack the desire to communicate with your partner and resolve important relationship issues.

To avoid being caught in the trap of this untrue destructive myth, you need to remember that love is the most powerful force in the universe. When you use your awesome power of love, there is absolutely no obstacle too big for you to overcome. The right solution for overcoming your relationship issues will be attracted to you.

Unfortunately this myth is incredibly easy to sneak into your unconscious mind. Men are particularly vulnerable because they often say and believe, "If this doesn't work, I'm out of here!" To guard against falling prey to this myth, I offer you a healthy, creative way of looking at your relationship – a way that can stop the fake myth dead in its tracks.

So, what you can do to stop the fake myth before it sneaks into your unconscious? First, call your imagination into action. Imagine your relationship like a beautiful garden that you are both planting together. You decide to make your garden lush and beautiful, so gorgeous that you want to maintain its beauty. To maintain its beauty, you decide to take the next step,

(Step 2) Weed the garden on a regular basis. Every day you check in on your garden and when there are weeds, you pluck them out. Of course, the weeds represent your issues and those heart warnings that something in the relationship needs adjusting. Because you are committed to the garden being beautiful, you are motivated to direct your passion to take you beyond fear and pain back to nurturing your precious relationship.

(Step 3) To further protect yourself, you want to safeguard your garden – make it impenetrable. A fun way that you and your partner can accomplish this is by daily repeating affirmations (positive thoughts) about your relationship. To make the most of the affirmations, you repeat them until they take root in the structure of your core beliefs. Affirmations (positive thoughts) might be ones like the following, "I love my partner just the way he or she is." "Together my partner and I are an awesome force." "The more I reveal my inner thoughts and feelings to my partner, the stronger we grow together."

Powerful thoughts repeated daily act like fertilizer to your garden. They nourish the flowers from the roots up. Having gratitude for your wonderful relationship is also highly beneficial for your garden. Gratitude acts like the sun shining down on your garden blessing it.

Now, I confess that using the garden analogy may seem a little feminine for many men. Well, even if it is, the process works so well that it is worth while going beyond little prejudices and using it. You might call your garden analogy your *secret marriage-works garden*. Remember, approximately 50% of marriages succeed, and you can be part of the positive statistics.

There is a second myth that is closely related to the first and it is important to understand this so you don't become victimized by it:

2. MYTH: Love is not enough!

TRUTH: This is a challenging one to overcome because it is extremely tempting to believe that *Love is not enough*. When there is a relationship issue bothering you, it is natural to want to fix it – to find solutions. You become like a relationship mechanic ready with your hammer and screw driver. For example, if you are a man and your female partner raises her voice and it is razor sharp and directed toward you, you automatically swing into action. Your male energy comes into play and you believe you can fix what is wrong by saying, "Sweetheart, no need to raise your voice. Everything will turn out fine." Your rational mind is telling you this is an excellent way to fix the situation. Well, is it?

Or, if you are a woman, you might decide to do your fixing in another way. You might say to your partner, "No need to raise your voice. There must be something bothering you. Let's get to the heart of it. Tell me what is really wrong." This is a woman's way of fixing and probably 99% of the time doesn't work. Well, is this right men? Does this type of fixing push you further away?

In both these cases the man and woman believe that *Love is not enough!* They want to fix what is wrong. Their rational mind has taken charge, forcing their intuitive Love Power to take a back seat.

When you believe that *love is enough*, you believe and act differently. You believe in the power of Love. Believing in the power of love means that when there is an issue (a conflict), you are willing to shut off your rational mind (your chatterbox). Instead, you are willing to say "No" to your rational Mind and to redirect your attention toward your Intuition, your Divine Spirit, your Love Power. *This is true love.* Love is activated when you surrender to the Divine Presence and intuitively know that it will guide you into doing what is right for you.

When you are in your love power, you are loving yourself for who you are and you are loving your partner for who he or she is. When your partner raises his or her voice, you will say something like this, "I hear you; I understand; and I am here for you." Something else you might do is to remain silent and from your heart send your partner love and caring. Thoughts and feelings travel invisibly at the speed of light and your partner will sense them. Thoughts are real!

When people turn to using their rational thinking mind as a way of demonstrating love, it is because deep down they fear their love is not enough to overcome relationship issues/barriers. They may also fear that deep down they don't deserve a loving, lasting relationship. The best way to let go of these types of fears is to begin with small steps. When there is a small issue, instead of trying to fix or mend it, leave it alone. Leave it alone and instead give your partner your caring, understanding and emotional support. You can do this silently, or by saying you understand their difficulty and are willing to listen. This will demonstrate to your partner that you love him or her, and are willing to be guided by your love power. You are standing powerfully in the force of love.

By taking small steps you will build confidence in your love and its power. Before long you will be excited about using your love power to overcome relationship issues. As part of your reward, you will discover that your relationship is on a more even keel and consequently there are not so many emotional rollercoaster ups and downs. When you really get good at standing in the *love power* and letting it be your relationship guide, you will feel on top of the world. You won't be tempted by myths like that of *"commitment is valid only as long as my relationship is good."*

You will know: *Love is enough! I am love. I am the force of love and I am using it!*

3. MYTH: Revealing what I really think leads to rejection.

TRUTH: When you express what you honestly think, you are revealing your *Spiritual "I" - the essence of your Divine Spirit.* You are claiming your right to be yourself and to be respected for who you are. No one can reject you except you! This may seem far out but is it? Let's explore!

It is true that a partner or sweetheart may not be attracted to you and will leave you! The good part of this is that it leaves you free and unencumbered to attract someone with whom you are compatible.

Risking revealing who you really are and expressing your authentic self can be a challenge. For women who have a history of believing they are subservient to men, this also means breaking through the race thought that women are the chattel property of men (many cultures still believe this).

What I have discovered from my coaching experience is that the majority of my clients report that the more frequently they express their real thoughts and risk rejection, (1) the less power the fear of rejection has over them, and (2) the more joy they have expressing their genuine thoughts and beliefs. After a while these people become their own best sales people because they have learned to trust their Divine Source – their Authentic Selves. Being *real* increases self-confidence.

4. MYTH: Men don't cry.

TRUTH: Men do cry. Men have feelings. When men feel safe and supported, they express their feelings. Men enjoy being appreciated for who they are and what they do. Trying to change or improve men tends to strip men of their self-confidence and power.

In today's world, women want men who express their emotions and are vulnerable. It is a woman's responsibility to create a supportive atmosphere, and lovingly help to make this possible.

5. MYTH: *Women don't know what they want.*

TRUTH: As Dr. John Gray says in his book, *MEN ARE FROM MARS, Women Are from Venus,* "When a woman is upset she needs time to explore her feelings before she is able to be her appreciative, accepting, and trusting self."

Many women aren't aware of what they want until they express their feelings. When a man listens to a woman express her feelings without trying to change her, she feels safe. Feeling safe and appreciated, most women tend to know exactly what they want and are excited to share their desires. It is important for women to be loved for who they are. Women want to inspire men and to have a good relationship.

6. MYTH: *In a lasting relationship, I will lose my identity.*

TRUTH: In a *lasting relationship,* two people function as a synergistic unit. The power of two joined happily together is greater than the power of one. To accomplish synergistic power, each person retains their personal identity, but their identities are enhanced by accepting and understanding their partners for who they are. When partners value each other, they support one another's growth and empower the love and passion which keeps the sparks flying and the relationship lively.

7. MYTH: Safe Sex is boring.

TRUTH: Fear is the absence of love or more aptly put, fear blocks you from feeling love. Practicing safe sex is a way to eliminate fear. Safe sex eliminates the fear of getting a sexually transmitted disease as well as eliminating the fear of getting pregnant - if that is a concern. Freed from fear, you are able to relax your muscles, feel good, and enjoy passionate love--making.

As part of your safe sex practices, you can (1) enjoy using condoms as a means ensuring worry-free love making and (2) enjoy an expanded definition of sex. If you haven't already discovered, you can explore and learn that orgasms frequently happen outside of intercourse. Orgasms can happen during mutual touching, in the joy of prolonged kissing and hugging, and also in other ways yet to be discovered together.

One expanded definition of sex that I like is: the enjoyment two people have experiencing the pleasures of loving and being loved. Although this definition may be stretching your imagination, I absolutely know of many instances where couples are not touching or even in the same physical space, and they are enjoying mutual orgasmic pleasure.

Safe sex can be a liberating, fun and exciting adventure – it is in your hands and your choice!

8. MYTH: Passion comes naturally.

TRUTH: Being passionate is an art that can be learned. Passion often springs to life when lit by an enthusiastic partner. Passion can lie dormant because a person doesn't know how to express it and is afraid of what will happen if they do express themselves. Also sometimes passion is asleep because your partner simply does not excite you. Below is an analogy that can help you when thinking about passion:

Passion=the logs
Passion afraid to express itself=wet logs
Passion ready to express itself=dry kindling logs
Passion expressing itself =dry logs which are lit and burning

The art of being passionate, including how to ignite your partner's passion, is explained in the practical guide books by Ellen Kreidman entitled *Light Her Fire* and *Light His Fire*. A quote from the author that I enjoy is, "Romance is a decision. Two keys to romance are: Be spontaneous and take a chance! Do what you fear most."

9. Opposites attract; like-minded people don't attract.

TRUTH: Opposites attract and like-minded people attract. Attraction depends on what makes you feel good – what *turns you on* and resonates *with you*. People who are attracted by opposites enjoy exploring their differences. People who are attracted by like-minded people enjoy exploring their similarities.

10. MYTH: There is something wrong with a man or woman who is not in a loving, lasting relationship.

TRUTH: A *lasting relationship* can be with one's self, with friends, with a sweet-heart, or with family. When a man or woman feels good about themselves, they are enjoying a fulfilling relationship. What matters is not how others judge you, but what you are experiencing as your truth.

I am often reminded of a quote from Gerald Jampolsky in his book, *Out of the Darkness, Into the Light*. He says, "Our purpose in relationships is just to see that spirit of love in each other, the light of love in everyone. That is the only reality."

Sexual Myths

1. Myth: Intimacy means good sex.

TRUTH: Intimacy means feeling close to your partner and being appreciated for the unique person you are. Much to the surprise of many men, and I am sure you know what I am talking about, intimacy does not mean "good sex". Being intimate requires that you feel emotionally close to your partner, and good sex can be an expression of intimacy, even though it is not intimacy itself. When you are having sex just for the fun of it, the sexual experience lacks that close bond between two people that inspires them to feel loved.

For sex to be intimate, it requires that
special ingredient of appreciation for each other.

Men are believed to be more physical than women and often equate sex with intimacy. Usually men don't feel loved when their sexual performance is lacking. Women, on the other hand, are generally more verbally expressive, emotional, and nurturing than men. They like to be listened to, heard, and told they are loved. Without these basic requirements being satisfied, women don't feel loved.

Men and women are both searching for love and appreciation;
the difference is in the way they typically experience being loved.

2. MYTH: I am no good as a man if I don't perform well sexually.

TRUTH: How a man values himself is more important that his sexual performance. When a man feels good about himself, he can express his genuine thoughts and feelings. He can go beyond his ego and the judgments of others and does not have to prove himself sexually according to presupposed standards. Most women desire and value a man who makes her feel special regardless of whether or not he can perform certain sexual acts. Women want men who can express their feelings and are vulnerable.

When you are ready to let go of the myth that a man is no good if he doesn't perform well sexually, then sex becomes an expression of love, joy and fun, *and not an expression of manhood!*

3. MYTH: Good sex is when my partner and I orgasm at the same time.

TRUTH: Good sex occurs when both partners are happy. You can be happy when you orgasm together, when you orgasm at different times, and even when you don't orgasm at all. Using safe sex practices, many couples enjoy orgasms in ways other than through intercourse. For instance, some people find their happiness while hugging and touching, and not by intercourse or even having an orgasm.

Believing that good sex occurs only when both partners orgasm simultaneously leads to *performance anxiety.* When you release yourself from this belief, then a good sexual experience (even without an orgasm) frees up your positive energy – your LOVE POWER. Now you can freely express your feelings of love, excitement, fun, and intimacy. What matters sexually is that you are happy with your choice of how you choose to experience sex.

Enjoyable sex happens when you take responsibility for your choices. As Bernie Zilbergeld said in *Male Sexuality,* "A good lover is not the one who already knows what to do but one who is open to learning about his partner's needs and desires."

A good lover listens to what their partner wants, and expresses his or her own desires. They are willing to take responsibility for their sexuality.

4. MYTH: I'm a lucky woman! I can fake orgasms.

TRUTH: "Many women experience a vague amorphous fear of losing themselves or of merging with their partners as they approach the somewhat egoless state of orgasm." says Lonnie Barbach, PhD, in her book, *For Each Other.*

Women who fake orgasms to please their partner as well as women who fake orgasms to quickly end their sexual experience are missing out. They are denying themselves pleasure and are being dishonest with their partners. Not only are they cheating themselves, but also their partners.

What I have found from clients is that women who fake orgasms over a prolonged period of time easily slip into believing that "all men want is sex." After all, why shouldn't they believe this when they are faking orgasms to be accepted rather than being truthful. If you are a woman reading this, perhaps this has happened to you or to a friend. Left unchecked, when a woman might continue to believe that all men want is sex, she will likely, in time, become resentful, lack passion, and have communication problems both inside and outside the bedroom.

Women who repeatedly fake orgasms are at risk of lying in bed like zombies, waiting for their partners to hurry up and finish. Rigid body language sends a message to their partner that something is wrong. He doesn't understand what it is, but does get the message that something is wrong with his performance and he is not pleasing his partner. Since a man equates good performance with being loved, he no longer feels loved. For both partners, if unchecked a vicious cycle of not feeling loved escalates and can wreck or cause havoc to a loving, lasting relationship.

5. MYTH: *It's wrong for the woman to be on top.*

TRUTH: The standards for what is right and wrong are either based on what you believe is proper or on what works for you. If you enjoy the man in the missionary position on top (which is less sexually assertive), then great. If you feel resistance about trying something different than the standard missionary position, you may want to take a look at why --- what thoughts you are having? Are you experiencing some fear? Many men fear losing their masculine power and control. Many women fear asking for what they want.

If you are acting out of fear, is this fear enslaving you? Fear has a way of creating a dam that blocks the flow of love and disconnects you from remembering that you are a spiritual being with unlimited *love power.*. Fear can be so destructive that Gerald Jampolsky titled one of his books, *Love is Letting Go of Fear.*

6. *MYTH: Pleasing my partner is more important than pleasing myself.*

TRUTH: Pleasing yourself is as important as pleasing your partner. When you try too hard, you build up resistance. Resistance is the silent culprit that pushes back your partner and can push your partner back so far that your he or she can no longer please you. What you believed was for good actually backfires.

If you find yourself trying too hard, here are a few tips to remember. Giving from an empty cup of pleasure creates stress. Giving from a full cup of pleasure gives joy.

You know you have reached your sexual heaven when you are giving that which you would like to receive.

TO GIVE JOY IS TO RECEIVE PLEASURE.

"We mistakenly assume that if our partners love us, they will react and behave in certain ways — the ways we react and behave when we love someone."
MEN ARE FROM MARS,
Women Are from Venus,

—Dr. John Gray

CHAPTER FIVE

Love Communication

What is Love Communication?

Although this example may not apply to you, you may know some people for whom this does apply:

Imagine you are attracted to someone who fulfills your best dreams. You fall deeply in love. The whole world is aglow. It seems like nothing can go wrong. Then, unexpectedly you awaken one day to discover your partner has taken off a mask. As you rub the magic fairy dust from your eyes, you discover yourself in an intimate relationship with a partner who you don't know well and with whom you have difficulty communicating. Suddenly you hurt. It seems that in one single stroke, you have fallen out of paradise and plunged into a dark, empty pit. You're stuck in the bottom of the pit. You want to climb out, but don't know how. Desperately you search for a rope to use as a lifeline.

Love communication supplies you with a rope you can use as your lifeline. It provides you with proven communication techniques that will free you from becoming a victim of your own feelings — controlled by feelings of anger, sadness, fear and regret.

Knowing you have a lifeline available is just what you need to give you the courage to achieve mastery over your negative feelings. Now you have access to the secrets enabling you to control your feelings, your destiny. By using the tools of love communication on a continuous basis, you can resolve relationship issues more quickly. If you are already married, mastering these tools will revive your marriage. You deserve to enjoy a marriage that works, and works successfully!

With these communication tools you can move yourself all the way from feelings of anger, back to your love. With practice, you will become an expert at releasing negative feelings and replacing them with positive ones. As your self confidence grows, more and more you will express your unwanted feelings, rather than keeping them bottled up and watching them fester. As Dr. John Gray suggests in his book, *What You Feel, You Can Heal*, "When you release pent-up negative feelings, you let go of the control they have over you, freeing you to heal your own hurt". Being free from hurt, you are able to experience that Divine serenity at the center of your Being. At peace, you regain control of your feelings and are able to attract experiences filled with joy and happiness.

When should you use Love Communication?

When you believe that someone other than yourself is *making you do something you don't want to do*, or you feel *controlled by anger, sadness or hurt*, it is time to take out your Love Communication tool kit. Let your negative feelings of anger, sadness or hurt act as your personal warning signals prompting you to take action. Your feelings will tell you when it is time to make a new decision. You have a choice:

1. to continue to indulge in your self-destructive negative thoughts or

2. to practice your communication tools until you have mastery over your negative thoughts and feelings.

In your Love Communication tool kit, you will discover two distinct sets of tools. *Set 1* is very safe and is most frequently used to support the woman when she is upset – it shows you a way to improve your communication with your partner. With practice, the rewards it offers is that you will enjoy a deeper level of shared emotional support, trust and acceptance.

Set 2 is the advanced set, where you share your intimate thoughts and feelings with your partner. With practice, the rewards it offers are outstanding: you will experience quantum growth and a new level of loving intimacy with your partner. You will feel that there is no obstacle too big for us to overcome!!!

While each tool set shares an identical core in the communication process, each is uniquely designed to fulfill different relationship needs. The safer technique is called the *Love Letter.* The advanced technique is called the *Advanced Love Communication technique.*

The safer Love Letter technique was developed by Dr. John Gray and described in his best selling book, *Men Are From Mars, Women Are from Venus.* Dr. Gray explains the Love Letter process in the chapter, *How to Communicate Difficult Feelings.* I will describe it in more detail later in this chapter. The Love Letter process consists of first writing a love letter, then a response letter, and afterwards sharing your feelings with your partner. The beauty of participating in this process is that it provides a safe haven while you are discharging the high impact of your negative emotions and exploring your own feelings. As part of the process, you will become more calm, centered and peaceful. It will feel as if your whole being is enveloped in a peaceful atmosphere.

As Dr. John Gray explains, "As men write letters they become more caring, understanding and respectful; as women write letters they become more trusting, accepting and appreciative."

The Love Letter technique is highly effective for the man who is in hibernation in his cave. It gives him a relationship tool to use that shows the way to listen to his own feelings in private. In his private space, he can continue emotionally supporting his partner while at the same time, he is working on mastering his own feelings. For the woman, the Love Letter is an effective way for her to become aware of her own feelings in private, and to do some self healing.

When you want to share your feelings with your partner, I recommend you use the *Advanced Love Communication.* where you communicate face-to-face with your partner. It is an effective verbal communication process using Dr. John Gray's Love Communication as its core foundation. The Advanced Love Communication technique is best used by couples who are secure in their relationship. Its advantages are:

1. it encourages spontaneous verbal expression of sensitive feelings,

2. it provides a way for both partners to listen, to be heard, and to be understand,

3. it is followed by immediate helpful feedback,

4. it takes into account nonverbal communication like tone of voice and facial expression and

5. it provides a way to resolve conflict and take new action focused on improving the love power and growth of your relationship.

The warning for using the Advanced Love Communication technique is that when using it, it is paramount to demonstrate respect for your partner. To illustrate what I mean, imagine you were a married couple. You were aware that listening to what your partner has to say is a vital part of the process. Next, imagine you were the husband requesting the encounter technique and were asking your wife to first listen to you.

This would require emotional support from your wife (and most women need emotional support themselves). Knowing this, before beginning the process you first invite your wife to participate. You invite your wife to participate by saying something like, "Are you prepared to listen and emotionally support me?" If your wife replies "No," the best thing for you to do would be to release her from your request. You need to accept that non-acceptance is your wife's privilege no matter what the reason is: She should not be asked to explain her motives.

Incidentally, for people in business, the love encounter is also an effective tool for resolving relationship conflict. Resolution enhances feelings of well being and safety which in turn increases productivity. As you would expect, when used in business, statements for expressing love, change from "I love you," to statements like: "I respect" and "I understand". Using this technique in business is equivalent to taking a quantum leap forward in long term success.

The Love Letter Technique

Using the love letter technique empowers you to feel better and respond more positively. As you express your pent up negative feelings, you discharge their high negative impact and consequently, their power over you is released. It is easy to replace old negative thoughts and feelings with new positive ones. Once you gain control over what you are thinking and feeling, your life experiences automatically reflect the changes. *Change your thoughts, change your life. Change your thoughts, change your relationships!!! THOUGHTS CREATE!!! Improved thoughts create improved relationships!!!*

The love letter technique is a powerful way for you to change your thoughts and and have that reflected in your relationship. It consists of three parts. They are:

1. Write a love letter expressing your feelings of anger, sadness, fear, regret and love.

2. Write a response letter expressing what you want to hear from your partner.

3. Share your love letter and response letter with your partner.

Although there are three parts, you have a choice. You can:

(1) do all three parts,

(2) parts one and two, or

(3) only part one or part two. If you want to accomplish having a more loving communication with your partner, you would choose doing parts one and two. If your main goal is to release

the high negative impact of your feelings, you would choose doing part one, or parts one and two. If you want to achieve a healing experience and improve your relationship, you would choose to do all three parts, including sharing your love letter with your partner. Examples follow illustrating how to use each part.

Part One: Writing A Love Letter

This love letter is primarily for your own benefit. Find a place that is private; a place where you can be alone and comfortable. When you are relaxed, preview the following steps for writing the first part of your love letter.

Step One: Address your letter to your partner. Pretend that your partner is listening to you with love, respect and understanding.

Step Two: Even if you are feeling sad or fearful, do your best to relax and move deeper into your feelings so you can access any underlying anger that may be producing feelings of sadness or fear. Often angry feelings are stored at a subconscious level, so you may not be able to consciously access them, but do your best. If you have some angry feelings, express them. Once expressed, move on to express feelings of sadness, fear, regret and love. For inspiration, look over the examples in this chapter under *Expressing Yourself.*

Step Three: Next write a few sentences about each of your feelings, expressing your feelings in simple language. Move through all your feelings, from anger to love.

Step Four: After expressing each feeling, pause and observe the next feeling as it comes up. Write about this feeling.

Step Five: Continue expressing your feelings until you have moved to the section where you are expressing your love. Be patient and allow yourself to feel the love in your heart.

Step Six: Sign your name at the end.

Step Seven: Take a few moments. Breathe in. Relax. Consider what it is that you want or need. Express your needs, wants, and desires in a P.S.

To help you understand how this works and to give you a working model, a sample situation and Love Letter from Dr. John Gray's book, *Men Are From Mars, Women Are From Venus* follows.

A Love Letter About Forgetfulness

When Tom napped longer than he had planned and forgot to take his daughter, Hayley, to the dentist, his wife Samantha was furious. Instead of confronting Tom with her anger and disapproval, Samantha decided to vent her feelings. She wrote the following Love Letter:

Dear Tom,

1. *ANGER:* I am furious that you forgot. I am angry you overslept. I hate it when you take naps and forget everything. You expect me to do everything. I am tired.

2. *SADNESS:* I am sad that Haley missed her appointment. I am sad you forgot. I am sad because I feel that I can't rely on you. I am sad you have to work so hard. I am sad that you are so tired. I am sad that you have less time for me. I feel hurt when you are not excited to see me. I feel hurt when you forget things. I feel that you don't care.

3. *FEAR:* I fear that I have to do everything. I am afraid to trust you. I fear that you don't care. I am afraid I will have to be responsible if something goes wrong. I don't want to do everything. I need your help. I fear needing you. I worry that you will never be responsible. I am terrified you are working too hard and you may get sick, even have a heart attack.

4. *REGRET:* I regret that I feel embarrassed when you miss appointments and are late. I am sorry that I am so demanding. I am sorry that I am not more accepting. I feel ashamed that I am not more loving. I am willing to accept who you are.

5. *LOVE:* I love you. I understand you were tired. You work so hard. I know you are doing your best. I forgive you for forgetting. Thank you for making another appointment with the dentist. Thank you for wanting to take Hayley to the dentist. I know in your heart you really do care. I know you love me. I feel so lucky to have you in my life. I want to share a romantic evening with you.

Love, Samantha

PS: In my heart I know you will be responsible to take Hayley next week to the dentist. I look forward to your positive reply.

Part Two: Writing a Response Letter

Writing the second part of the love letter called the response letter is healing. When the woman writes the Response Letter, she opens herself up to receive the love and emotional support of her male partner. When the man writes his Response Letter, he opens himself up to receive the trust, appreciation and acceptance of his female partner.

In writing your response letter, imagine that you are your partner and then write as you would like your partner to respond to what you have said. Include all the things you would like to hear from your partner about the hurts you have received. The following lead-in phrases can be helpful in getting you started:

Thank you for...

I understand...

I am sorry...

You deserve...

I want...

I love...

Next is an example of a response letter written by Samantha, who is imagining that she is her husband, Tom. Notice she writes what she wants to hear.

Dear Samantha,

Thank you for loving me so much. Thank you for sharing your feelings. I understand that it hurts you when I am forgetful, don't pick up after myself, and miss appointments. I am sorry that I don't offer to help you more often. You deserve my support, my understanding, and I want to help you more often. I do love you, and I am so honoured and happy that you are my wife.

I love you,
Paul

Part Three: Sharing Your Love And Response Letters

Sharing your letters is important for couples as it offers the following:

- An opportunity for your partner to support you.
- A way for you to receive the understanding you need and deserve.
- A process to give feedback to your partner in a loving and respectful way
- A method to increase your intimacy and passion.
- A way for your partner to learn what is important to you and how to support you.
- Effective tools to use when communication breaks down.
- A safe way to express and hear negative feelings – *Super important!*

Five Different Ways of Sharing Your Love and Response Letters

There are five different ways for you and your partner to share your love and response letters. You will want to choose the way that is best for both of you. Examples of the five ways follows:

1. *He* reads her love and response letters out loud while his partner is present. Then he holds her hands and expresses his own loving response with a greater awareness of what she needs to hear.

2. *She* reads her love and response letters out loud while her partner is listening. Then as he holds her hands, she expresses her own loving response with a great awareness of what she

needs him to hear. (Note the difference between *1* and *2* is who reads the letters.)

3. First *he* reads her response letter out loud to her. Next he reads her love letter out loud. By first learning what his wife/partner wants, it makes it easier for him to hear her negative feelings as he reads them in the love letter. After reading his partner's love letter, the man holds his partner's hands and offers his own loving response with greater awareness of what she needs to hear.

4. First *she* reads her response letter out loud to her partner. Next *she* reads her love letter out loud. The process is the same as in *3* except that *she* reads the response and love letters.

5: *She* gives her letters to him and *he* reads them privately within a certain time frame; e.g., twenty four hours. When finished, he thanks his partner. With greater awareness of her needs, he gives her a loving response.

What To Do If Your Partner Can't Respond Lovingly

Some men and women have great difficulty participating in writing and hearing love letters. If this is the case, they should be excused from reading them.

Be aware that even when a partner chooses to hear a letter, sometimes he or she is not able to respond in a loving manner, at least at that time. Let's take the example of Paul and Teresa.

If Paul is not responding more lovingly after he has heard his partner's letters, it maybe because he is upset and not capable. He may feel attacked and hurt by his wife's anger and become defensive. Most likely Paul needs time to relax and reflect on what was said.

Sometimes when a person hears a Love Letter they only hear the anger and this shields them from hearing the love. In such cases, it helps if the person takes a break and then reads the letter a second time, particularly the regret and love sections.

Let's imagine a husband is upset after reading a love letter. He could respond with his own love letter that would enable him to process the negative feelings that his partner expressed. One man confided in me, "Sometimes I don't know what is bothering me until my wife shares a love letter, and then suddenly I have something to write about. By writing my own love letter, I am able to discover what my own thoughts and feelings are and am then able to get back in control of my emotions. Then, when I again read my wife's love letter, I can hear the love beneath her hurt."

If a man cannot immediately respond with love, he needs to know that it is okay and he will not be punished. To give himself time out and still support his partner, he can say something like, "Thank you for writing your letter. I need some time to think about it and then we can talk." It is important in this case that the husband does not share critical feelings about his wife's letter. Sharing letters with your partner needs to be safe.

The above suggestions for sharing letters also applies when a woman has difficulty responding to a man's love letters. I generally recommend that couples read the letters they have written out loud. I find that reading your partner's letter out loud helps your partner feel loved.

Have fun experimenting with the different methods and making a decision about which method is best suited for you.

When To Write Love Letters

The ideal time to write a Love Letter is when you are upset and want to feel better. You can write love letters to:

1. An intimate partner

2. A friend, child or family member

3. A business associate or a client. You would replace the words "I love you" with "I appreciate" and "I respect." In most cases these letters are not shared.

4. Yourself.

5. God or a Higher Power.

6. Yourself but reverse roles.. If it is hard to forgive someone, pretend that you are that person and you will be amazed at how quickly you are able to start forgiving.

7. A monster. If you are very upset and your feelings are mean, vent them in a letter. Then burn the letter. If the letter is written to your partner, do not expect your partner to read it unless you can both handle the negative feelings.

8. An absent or dead person. When something that happens reminds you of unresolved feelings from childhood, use your imagination to go back in time and write a letter to one of your parents (or whomever caused you to be upset). Share your feelings and ask for support.

Why We Need To Write Love Letters

To achieve healthy, loving relationships, women need to be able to share their feelings and feel supported, understood, and respected. Men need to feel appreciated, accepted and trusted. I believe most women will agree that is very challenging for a woman when she shares her upset feelings and, as a result, her partner feels unloved. Right women?

Of course. sharing the love letters and being vulnerable can also be challenging for the man. His partner's negative feelings may sound critical, blaming, demanding and resentful. As a result he may reject his woman's feelings, and then she ends up joining him in feeling unloved.

To be successful in your relationship requires two essential ingredients:

1. a man's ability to listen lovingly to a woman's feelings, and
2. a woman's ability to share her feelings in a loving and respectful way. Both these ingredients need to be working, and working well!

In a healthy relationship, partners communicate their thoughts and feelings. To expect perfect communication is too idealistic. Fortunately somewhere in-between, there is ample room for happiness and a desire to grow as a couple.

Realistic Expectations

It is unrealistic to expect that communication will always be easy. It is realistic to expect that communication has its ups and downs. Some feelings are difficult to express without potentially hurting your partner. Couples who have wonderful and loving relationships will sometimes agonize over how to communicate in a way that works. It is often difficult to understand another person's point of view; particularly when the person is saying something that your heart and gut tells you is not what you want to hear. It is challenging to show respect to that person when your own feelings are raw.

Many couples mistakenly believe that their inability to communicate successfully is a reflection of their lack of love for each other. That is not the truth. Do you know why? Effective communication is a skill and requires education. Fortunately it is a skill that can be learned and practised. Repeated practice absolutely makes a huge difference. With practice you can expect great improvement and will understand that it is always possible to get back to the love..

Advanced Love Communication

Face-To-Face Communication: The Ultimate Tool For Keeping Your Intimacy Alive And Prospering

You have probably heard the expression "Love is the greatest force in the Universe. With enough love all things are possible."

You may be one of those people who has good reason to doubt the validity of that expression. "After all" you might ask yourself,: "How can you use this great thing called love when you are angry with your partner, upset that you are experiencing a loss of freedom, and miserable that your partner doesn't seem to care?"

This is the DYNAMITE QUESTION. I believe you will discover the answer as you learn how to use love power and love communication tools. Without workable communication tools many couples drift apart emotionally. They end up feeling as if they are stuck at the bottom of a bottomless pit from which they can't escape. With these communication tools however; couples feel reassured that they have a proven way to resolve a relationship crisis, trusting the power of their love, and deepening their intimacy.

As a workshop facilitator for Dr. John Gray, author of *Men are From Mars, and Women are From Venus,* I witnessed first-hand the miracle of *Advanced* Love Communication saving relationships that were on the brink of disaster. In my own private practice as a relationship therapist, I witnessed couples who were at odds with each other break through relationship barriers to again share love, happiness, and intimacy. I like to think of *Advanced* Love Communication as a *DREAM MAKER.*

"And how does *Advanced* Love Communication make dreams?" you might ask. I believe Love Communication is a *Dream Maker* because it enables the couple's dreams of loving, cherishing one another, and *living happily after* to come true.

Are you interested in learning more about *Advanced* Love Communication as it is used face-to-face with your partner?

To begin, *Advanced* LOVE COMMUNICATION has two parts. The first part is Dr. John Gray's communication process of moving from anger to love. Dr. Gray has given me permission to use his technique, and for this I am most thankful. The process of moving from anger to love forms the central core of the *Advanced* LOVE COMMUNICATION and is proven to be highly successful.

Because learning *Advanced* LOVE COMMUNICATION is an exciting adventure, I believe you will want to prepare yourself. What follows are some check-in questions. The first set of questions is for the partner who will be expressing feelings, and the second set is for the partner who is actively listening.

Now for my heart-felt warning: If you or your partner answer any of the questions with a "No" response, I recommend you put the *Advanced* LOVE COMMUNICATION process on hold. You can do it later. Start off with Dr. John Gray's love letter technique instead. It will provide you with excellent emotional support, guidance, and courage.

When you and your partner have answered the ten following "Check-In Questions" affirmatively, you can be reassured that, "You are ready to start sharing your *Advanced* Love Communication!"

Check-In Questions
For the Partner Expressing Feelings

In sharing my feelings with my partner, do I believe:

1. My partner loves me for who I am?

2. It is safe for me to express my angry feelings to my partner?

3. That my partner will emotionally support me?

4. If my partner has difficulty listening and supporting me, that I can handle it?

5. That my partner is committed to the success of our relationship?

6. That I am committed to the success of our relationship?

7. Is it important that both my partner and I are happy?

8. My partner and I form an intimate whole in which my partner reflects back to me what I need to further my growth?

9. I am willing to take responsibility for my thoughts and feelings?

10. I am willing to make changes and create *New Thoughts* and *Feelings* that I will practice and integrate into my relationship?

Check-In Questions
For the Partner Who Is Actively Listening

In listening to my partner's feelings, do I believe that:

1. My partner loves me for who I am?

2. I am willing to listen to my partner even if my partner expresses angry feelings toward me?

3. I am able to emotionally support my partner?

4. I can ask for what I need even if I have difficulty listening to, or emotionally supporting, my partner?

5. My partner is committed to the success of our relationship?

6. I am committed to the success of our relationship?

7. Is it important that both my partner and I are happy?

8. My partner and I are part of an intimate whole in which I help through listening and reflecting back to my partner what my partner needs for growth?

9. I am willing to take responsibility for my feelings and reactions?

10. I am willing to make changes and create *New Thoughts* and *Feelings* that I will practice and integrate into my relationship?

As a listener, please first read the section called "What To Do As The Listener" that follows the Love Encounter Technique on page 113.

Advanced Love Communication

Moving From Anger to Love

Before you begin the process, I want to reassure you that it is perfectly normal to feel scared. So take a deep breath and relax. You are not alone. I am here to reassure you that every couple for whom I have done marriage coaching feels much better after they have completed the Advanced Love Communication process. It is such a relief to express pent up feelings and have a partner who is willing to listen and emotionally support you. This is part of the commitment and is taken seriously. So, take another deep breath, relax more, and know you will be safe and emotionally supported as you express your feelings.

Honestly, I believe every couple on earth has experienced being angry with his or her partner. That is why this step-by-step process is so important. You need to know how to safely express your anger followed by a proven way to return to sharing love with your partner.

Once you have succeeded, you will feel great, probably euphoric. Please, don't stop there. Whenever you feel angry (or have negative feelings) repeat the process. Soon the steps will become automatic and you will find yourself using them in the ways that are most helpful for you. For me, I often go through the steps silently until I reach an inner feeling of peace and love.

As part of the process of moving from anger to love, both you and your partner will take turns expressing yourselves. To create clarity, you can name yourselves Partner A and Partner B. First, Partner A will express each of the emotional states starting with Level 1, that is anger which moves all the way through to, and completing Level 5, which is love. Partner B will be the active listener.

If you are Partner A, you may want to begin your sentences by using a suggested lead-in phrase like the one for anger: "I resent...". An example of what you might say is, "I resent the mean tone of voice you use when you talk to me."

Following the instructions for *active listening,* there is an example of a real a*dvanced* LOVE COMMUNICATION, *From Anger to Love,* that took place between Laura and Jim.. Check it out! It is intended to be inspiring, so it will inspire you.

Now, it is time to begin. Please go to the next page. This will make it easier in case you want to copy the page.

From Anger to Love

For the Partner Expressing Feelings, please follow this process:

Begin by saying to your partner, "I am sharing my feelings with you and I appreciate your listening."

It is important to be there 100% for your partner. Now complete expressing your emotions from the Anger all the way through to the Love.

You can use the lead-in phrases to help you express each emotion; e.g. "I don't like it ..."

Level 1: **For ANGER**

I don't like it...

I resent...

I feel frustrated...

I am angry that...

I feel furious...

I am annoyed...

Level 2: **For SADNESS**

I feel disappointed...

I am sad that...

I feel hurt...

I wanted...

I want...

Level 3: **For FEAR**

It is painful...

I feel worried...

I am afraid...

I feel scared...

I need...

Level 4: **For REGRET**

I regret that...

I feel embarrassed...

I am sorry...

I feel ashamed...

I didn't want...

I am willing ...

Level 5: **For LOVE**

> I love...
>
> I want to...
>
> I appreciate...
>
> I forgive...
>
> I thank you for...
>
> I understand...
>
> I trust....
>
> I know....

When Partner A has finished expressing feelings from anger through to love, it is time to receive feedback from Partner B. Take your time. Next Partner B will express his or her feelings to Partner A and then receive feedback from Partner A. The roles are reversed.

In most instances, after the sharing, both partners will experience a warm bonding. If this is true for you, you have the green light to proceed with the exercises and continue for three more levels to *Level 8*. This gives you an opportunity to express the impact of the new feelings of love you are experiencing and the positive action you are willing to take to deepen your intimacy. You are letting your partner know how you will let love work for both of you.

I call this *The LOVE ENCOUNTER TECHNIQUE* and I developed it as a way of deepening intimacy.

The Love Encounter Technique – Adding to the love communication you just completed

You will begin by again saying to your partner: "Once again I am going to express my feelings and would appreciate your listening."

Level 6: **For: WHAT LOVE DOES FOR ME**

As I feel listened to ......

As I am acknowledged....

Feeling understood, I....

When I feel appreciated...

Knowing I am forgiven...

When I am trusted...

When I feel our love, I....

As I feel safe to express myself...

Level 7: **For: WHAT LOVE DOES FOR OUR RELATIONSHIP**

As our relationship is freed from fear, I ...

I love it when ...

I experience...

My spirit ....

Now I believe our relationship will ....

With the deepening of our love ....

Level 8: **For: POSITIVE ACTION I AM WILLING TO TAKE**

I intend to ...

At a spiritual level, I accept ....

I choose to ...

I affirm that ....

I am excited to ....

I passionately ....

I give you my word that...

I willingly change ...

So that you end your session in a healthy, positive way, say to your partner, "Thank you for listening."

A respectful response from your partner would be something like, "You are welcome. I appreciate you!"

After you and your partner have shared the entire process, it is time to give one another feedback. Usually this feedback is so inspiring and supportive that you will experience a quantum leap in your trust and intimacy.

What To Do As The Listener

Listening is a skill that can be developed. To become a good listener you need to learn how to be a disciplined observer – an observer who has the courage to be objective and remain *emotionally detached* from what is being said. This means that you will be able to control your own feelings of anger, fear and sadness. Being the master of your feelings empowers you to resist responding to your partner with criticism, blame or put-downs.

As a listener, when you feel attacked by your partner, here is a good "self-talk" technique my clients like to use to stay in control of their emotions. You are invited to use it. Pretend that the attack by your partner is like an arrow that has been aimed to hit and shatter you where you are most vulnerable. We call this your *inner vulnerable self* and you can speak to it. Say, "What my partner is saying is not *me*. What my partner is expressing is a mirror image of my partner's inner thoughts. I choose to stay aware of what my partner is expressing. I have faith that my observations will reveal the inner thoughts and beliefs causing my partner's experiences. Once my partner recognizes what thoughts are causing the unwanted experiences, my partner can change the thoughts. Of course I know that a change in thoughts will automatically change the experiences.

By trusting that my partner cares about me, I open myself to listen without judgement to my partner's deeper longings. As I enhance my understanding of my partner, I learn more about myself.

There is a second excellent "self-talk" technique that is actually fun to use when you feel attacked by your partner and your *inner vulnerable self* keeps trying to interrupt you while you are listening. The technique is to say something like this to your *inner vulnerable self:* "Okay Mr. Chatterbox, step aside! I am in charge. What my partner says is important, and I intend to listen."

Now, if Mr. Chatterbox continues to interrupt, say, "I hear what you are saying, but it is not your turn to talk. I'll write down your complaint and address it later. I need to stay focused on my listening, so please exit the front door. Thank you. Good-bye." If you are good at visualizing, you can visualize Mr Chatterbox exiting the front doors you close them behind him.

As you listen to your partner, I recommend taking notes. Notes will help you stay focused and keep your attention off of Mr. Chatterbox. The notes will be helpful giving supportive feedback to your partner. Following are examples:

✓ Statements that were repeated.

✓ Emotional statements.

✓ Statements that reflect a pattern.

✓ Statements that relate to the past.

✓ Times when you feel threatened.

✓ Areas in which you believe your partner may want to change.

✓ Statements your partner made that you believe were not true.

✓ Areas you believe a change for both of you would enhance your intimacy.

It is important when giving feedback to face your partner and look into your partner's eyes. This reaffirms your sincerity and honesty. Oh! And be sure to tell your ego to be quiet.

When finished giving your partner feedback, discuss whether or not you want to switch roles. Be truthful. If you decide affirmatively, Partner B would speak and Partner A would listen. If the woman has gone first, she may choose to linger in the feelings of emotional support given by her partner. Often stopping after the woman expresses her feelings produces better results than quickly changing roles. If this is what the woman chooses, the male partner may opt to use Dr. John Gray's Love Letter Technique, or patiently wait until the woman is ready to listen. In making this particular decision, it is important the woman feels cared for, respected and understood. If the man has expressed first, it is important that he feels appreciated, accepted and trusted.

If you believe that you are not being successful, this is a strong indication that you are confused and would gain clarity by consulting with your inner source as described in the first of the *Ten Love Powers* in Chapter Three.

An Example Of Advanced Love Communication

To help you better understand how the process works, here is an example of the LOVE COMMUNICATION, *Moving From Anger to Love*. Notice how the partners express their feelings. The woman expresses her feelings followed by her partner expressing his feelings. When the man finishes, the woman indicates that she is feeling comfortable. With both partners feeling good, they decide to continue. The woman then continues the LOVE COMMUNICATION expressing her feelings through *Level 8*. Here she relates the Positive Action in her relationship that she is willing to take. You can sense both the man and woman's joy and feelings of success as they complete the last three levels of communication.

Laura's Love Communication—From Anger to Love

Laura feels she has become like a mother to her partner. This is how she expresses her feelings:

ANGER: I feel like your Mother constantly picking up your clothes and other junk scattered all over the house. I am overwhelmed by these duties along with being treated like your memory bank. You count on me to remember your appointments and find your junk whenever you misplace it – which is frequently. I am sick and tired of you using me. I resent being treated like your mother.

SADNESS: I am sad you treat me this way. It hurts me that you treat me more like a Mother more than a lover. I work so hard and all I get for all my hard work is being treated like a Mother. I don't feel safe to tell you what I feel and when I need to be nurtured. I am totally drained. I wish I knew what to do.

FEAR: I'm worried that I am going to end up an old worn out nag, look ugly: someone you no longer want. I'm scared you will wake up one day and no longer find me attractive. I need your help and understanding.

REGRET: I am sorry that I can't always return your love. I regret I can't seem to move past my feelings of being overwhelmed. I feel ashamed and am willing to try to change.

LOVE: I love and appreciate your compassion and caring for me. I want to resolve our issues. I appreciate your listening to me. I forgive you for not picking up after yourself. We need to define our duties. You are getting better at picking up after yourself. Thank you for your patience. I want us to share more joy and laughter. I understand you are trying, but just don't know what to do. I trust our love will see us through our relationship issues.

Jim's Love Communication—From Anger to Love

Jim feels cut off and put down by his partner, Laura. He feels a loss of manhood. This is how Jim expresses his feelings:

ANGER: I hate it when you raise your voice to get your point across. Every time you disagree with me, you say I'm arguing. That really turns me off. I'm frustrated. I get furious because I feel that you humor me so you can sneakily criticize me and put me down. You don't respect me or what I have to say.

SADNESS: I am very disappointed. I can't seem to be romantic and often don't feel passionate. I'm sad you are not satisfied with what we have, and that your happiness seems to depend upon our always having something more.

FEAR: It pains me to watch you struggle so hard to achieve things. I am worried that having to be successful controls you and that you can never be happy. Sometimes I am scared we won't be able to get back to the love. I need to know I am appreciated and trusted no matter how difficult our situation may seem.

REGRET: I am embarrassed when in public you talk about all you do for us. I am sorry and ashamed I have not been a better provider and lover. I am willing to change.

LOVE: I love you for all your wonderful feminine qualities, for being compassionate and caring. I love your little girl that peeps out from inside you. Your playfulness makes me want sex more often. I appreciate all you do for me. I forgive you for cutting me off and not providing a safe place for me to express myself. Thank you for loving me. I trust that our issues will disappear as we practice our communication skills.

After Laura and Jim finished expressing their feeling from *Anger to Love* in *Level 5*, Jim asked Laura if she wanted to continue to *Level 8*. Laura said that she did want to continue because she believed the last three levels would make her more secure in her feelings of being loved.

Laura then asked Jim if he wanted to continue. Jim said he believed this would bring them together in emotional bonding to a place where they could take positive action in deepening their love and intimacy. Jim agreed with Laura that they continue sharing.

In agreement, Laura and Jim continue sharing. Notice how Laura and Jim are in synch in the last three levels.

Laura's Love Communication—Through to Taking Positive Action

WHAT LOVE DOES FOR ME: When you listen to me, I feel warm and safe and again believe life is exciting. As I am understood, I feel good about me. As I am forgiven, I feel safe. When you demonstrate to me that you trust me, I feel secure and am filled with energy. When I know that I am loved I feel warm, cozy, passionate and like sharing.

WHAT LOVE DOES FOR OUR RELATIONSHIP: As our relationship is freed from fear, I feel very close to you and want to share my deepest thoughts and secrets with you. I love it when you appreciate my compassion and little girl. I am happy that you want to be with me. I am deeply grateful and thankful. Now I believe our relationship will soar!

POSITIVE ACTION: I intend to be more loving, to be more aware of what I am saying, and to replace my negative thoughts and feelings with positive ones. I choose to take responsibility for what happens to me. I affirm that I am going to give myself permission to be more passionate. I am happy to change for the love we share.

Jim's Love Communication—Through to Taking Positive Action

WHAT LOVE DOES FOR ME: I feel validated when I know I am loved. As I am understood, I feel you are there for me. As you appreciate me, I feel more like a man. When I am forgiven, I feel a weight lifted and a new sense of oneness with you. When I am trusted, I feel more like a man, successful, and a good provider. When I feel our love, I feel like an eagle soaring high in the sky.

WHAT LOVE DOES FOR OUR RELATIONSHIP: When I no longer feel like I am walking on pins and needles in our relationship, I again trust you. I love it when you are happy and joyful in spite of all that goes wrong. I experience tremendous harmony and peace when we are aligned. I feel like I am one with God and I can achieve anything to which I set my mind.

POSITIVE ACTION: I intend to listen before I spout unsolicited advice. I promise to do my best to pick up after myself and to remember. I spiritually accept our unity and Divine Beingness. I willingly take responsibility for my thoughts and actions. I affirm that I love you with all my heart, Laura. I give you my word that I will do my best to understand you. My word is my bond. I joyfully change for the better. I love you now and forever!

Taking Positive Action, From Anger to Love

Because every person is unique and different, it seems inevitable that couples will differ in their opinions, and experience disagreements. Unfortunately the disagreements end up in arguments and when they heat up, partners loose control of their emotions. They feel anger, fear, resentment, sadness. Feeling cut off from their love, it feels like they have fallen into a pit of despair from which escape is impossible. The worst part is that the couple feels hopeless. Although both partners experience anger, the real source of the anger is not knowing how to climb out of a situation that seems hopeless. That is where LOVE COMMUNICATION comes to the rescue. It is the escape ladder that can be used to climb out of what seems like a hopeless pit of despair.

Knowing how LOVE COMMUNICATION works,
and using it, is vital to having a marriage-that-works!

As a partner, not knowing how to get back to the love you once shared creates feelings of hurt and sadness. Underneath these feelings, anger is mounting. Sometimes this anger is directed toward the partner, sometimes toward self, and sometimes toward self and partner.

To avoid going down a slippery slope and falling prey to a pit of hopeless despair, partners can choose to use *ADVANCED* LOVE COMMUNICATION. Making this choice, couples give themselves the opportunity to explore their differences and deepen their understanding, intimacy, and self-growth. Instead of being something bad and hurtful, differences of opinion and disagreements can be the catalyst for stepping up one's relationship and enjoying a deeper intimacy, love and respect.

In the process and as you work through your disagreements, it is important to work all the way from expressing your feelings of anger, sadness, fear, and regret back to feelings of love. To take full advantage of the *ADVANCED* LOVE COMMUNICATION, it is important to share your positive intentions in taking positive action as part of *ADVANCED* LOVE COMMUNICATION.

The three steps of taking positive action are: What Love Does For Me, What Love Does for Our Relationship, and Positive Action.

Because every thing you do begins with a single thought, your thoughts always create what happens to you. When you change your thoughts, you change what happens to you. The results of changing your thoughts are profound. By changing your thoughts, you can achieve a relationship that mirrors your deepest desires. It can be a relationship filled with love, intimacy, joy, fun, happiness and adventure; *plus*, it can last forever.

Because *ADVANCED* LOVE COMMUNICATION is the tool that assures you can achieve and keep your dream relationship, when you have completed its exercises, you deserve to congratulate yourself. You have proven that you can move from thoughts of anger to thoughts of love and taking positive action.

Words that I wrote and like to say to myself that inspire success when using the *ADVANCED* LOVE COMMUNICATION techniques follow. I invite you to join me.

God Expressing As Me is Divine

My Mind is the Center of Divine Creation
and has provided within me a pattern of exquisite perfection
that acts as my guide working for me as I work with it.
As I consciously connect and surrender to my Divine Guide,
I easily uproot negative thoughts and patterns
replacing them with new thoughts and beliefs -
thoughts and beliefs that are loving and in harmony with those
*   of my partner.*

Adventuring on our life journey together, my partner and I
grow and prosper in an orderly sequence of creative thinking and growth
that is far greater and more magnificent than we ever imagined possible.

For all of this including my LOVE POWER and LOVE
*   COMMUNICATION, I give thanks.*
I know that growth, fulfillment, love and intimacy with my partner
are alive and prospering.

All Is Well!

CHAPTER SIX

Change Your Thoughts, Change Your Relationships

"Beliefs are simply repeated thoughts with strong feelings attached to them. A belief is when you have made up your mind, the verdict is in, you've nailed the door shut and thrown away the key, and there is no room for negotiation."
—Rhonda Byrne, "How *The Secret* Changed My Life"

Your Handy Relationship Tool Kit

Do you harbor some negative beliefs about your partner? If you answer *No*, you likely need to re-examine your answer.

*"Sometimes a **decision** you made when you were a child morphs into a belief that jeopardizes your whole life."*
—Dr. Melba Burns, author of "Don't Retire, Refire!"

Negative beliefs develop over time. When you have held them for a long while, they become friends who are guiding your life. Sometimes the guidance is conscious and sometimes it is unconscious. Most often you follow the guidance automatically and don't question it. When you stop and take time to examine your beliefs you will undoubtedly find many that are causing you pain - even sabotaging your relationship. Fortunately you have an opportunity to go back to the negotiating table and have a frank discussion with yourself about your decision making. You, and you alone, have the power to change your beliefs by changing your thoughts. Of course, when you change your thoughts you automatically change what is happening in your relationship.

When you go to the negotiating table with a set of handy tools to assist you, the process of making changes can be fun and exciting. For example, you can try out a new *thought* and watch the effect it has on you and your relationship. If you don't like the result, you can go back to the negotiating table and create a different thought – a different outcome. I recall in the book called *The Secret* by the author Rhonda Byrnes, that Michael Bernard Beckwith claims that one good positive thought has more power than a thousand negative thoughts. That is why one good positive thought replacing an old pattern of beliefs can totally transform your relationship (your marriage) from one that is not working to a relationship (marriage) that is fulfilling and working.

If you are having doubts because you have already been through therapy or read self-help books and your relationship is still not working for you, you deserve to know the true reason you continue to have issues. The reason is that you have made no mental changes so you are creating the same issues over and over again. Desiring a new outcome, many people have even left their partner, and found a new one only to discover they are again facing the same issues. Of course the reason for this is not the new partner, but rather that the partner making the change has created the same issues. Remember, wherever you go, you take yourself with you! Until you make a change, your relationship issues will get bigger and more intense. It is as if your issues have a voice of their own warning you to change, and if you don't listen and comply they will make things worse.

For everything that happens in your relationships, there is a causal thought pattern that precedes and maintains your experience. Your consistent thinking patterns create your experiences. When you really *get* that it is your thought patterns that create your relationship experiences, then you can stop blaming your partner, your relationship, and other people for what you don't like. Instead, by tapping the awesome power within yourself, you can take full responsibility for creating a satisfying relationship. Because the old thought patterns are attached to your needs and they may be hiding in disguise below the level of your conscious awareness, your willingness to make a change is necessary.

Using your relationship tool kit, you can make the choice to change and grow with your new thoughts, or to stay comfortable in the repetitive outcomes your old thoughts create. As long as you are consciously making a choice, you are in charge of your destiny.

Because I believe actions speak louder than words, I am going to share with you an example of how changing your old beliefs to *new thoughts* works. The example is about a single woman wanting to attract her ideal partner.

Betty is a popular single woman who attracts many men. Every time she starts dating someone special, her old lover named Jerry calls her. Jerry acts so sweet and understanding that Betty wants him. However, sweet as Jerry is, Betty despises Jerry for dangling in front of her the carrot of a long-term relationship. He will not commit to Betty's request that they share a long term relationship. Jerry's behaviour confuses Betty. Part of her wants Jerry, while another part despises him.

Betty and Jerry are interesting because both of them are suffering pain. At the moment, however, their pain is acceptable because it provides a way for them to continue their fear of intimacy at a subconscious level. Once they become aware of how their pain is serving them to avoid intimacy, they can make changes. They can choose:

1. To share their new awareness and work together to achieve intimacy, or

2. To separate and move on to new situations that resonate with their desires.

Issues such as *fear of intimacy* are what I refer to as *Relationship Barriers*. As the example illustrates, breaking through relationship barriers is a choice. Making a conscious decision to either change to a new *thought,* or to stay in your old habit pattern of beliefs, is a choice. Deciding to change your old habit patterns takes guts and a willingness.

As far as being happy, what matters is that you respect your choice. When you consciously choose your relationship experiences, you can expect your self-confidence to grow and your ability to deal with your fears to be far greater. You will then be able to perceive problems not as obstacles, but rather as opportunities for growth. Keeping this in mind, the most important thing you can do for yourself as you learn how to change old habit patterns to *new thoughts* is to have fun as you make conscious choices.

Relationship issues represent all those reasons why you *can't, won't and are not* enjoying a satisfying, fulfilling relationship. The reasons may be buried in your subconscious thinking so you may not be aware of them. If you are having difficulty making and keeping a commitment to achieve a loving, lasting relationship, or are unhappy in a long-term relationship, this is an excellent indication that you are up against a barrier of relationship issues.

AN IMPORTANT REMINDER: The greater your fear, the greater your resistance to change. The greater your resistance to change, the harder you must work to maintain your relationship barriers (issues). With a willing attitude to change, your tool kit will guide you on *how* to make your relationship dreams come true.

Replacing Old Belief Patterns With New Thoughts

Your Pocket-sized Relationship Toolkit

This pocket-sized relationship toolkit is yours! When you are up against relationship issues you want to change, repeat your *new thought* several times daily. For best results, I suggest you write out your *new thought* on a 3 X 5 inch index card and stick it somewhere handy such as on your bathroom mirror, on your car dashboard, or by your bedside.

Continue repeating your *New Thought* until it replaces your old belief, and you are experiencing a positive change in your relationship.

Normally this takes six weeks; however, when you are enthusiastic, change happens more rapidly. Repeat your *new thoughts* until they become new habits that trigger your success.

There are more than fifty relationship issues (barriers) that I have identified. The *new thoughts* that I have selected to overcome and replace the old belief patterns have been tested and proven in several groups over a period of twenty *plus* years. As you browse through the relationship barriers, you will be attracted to those that can make a difference in your relationship. Notice if a pattern arises in the barriers you have selected.

In your Relationship Tool Kit that follows, each relationship barrier is identified by the belief that creates and sustains the barrier.

REMEMBER: *The way to change a relationship barrier is to repeat the new thought until it becomes habit and you notice a positive change in your relationship.*

50 PLUS RELATIONSHIP BARRIERS AND YOUR TOOLS FOR OVERCOMING THEM

ABANDONMENT

BELIEF: I have been rejected and left out. I feel betrayed, fearful, and hurt. It is hard for me to trust again.

NEW THOUGHT: I let go of feeling rejected and replace my feelings with understanding, compassion and forgiveness. I am open to understanding my pain, what thoughts I had to cause my pain, and to forgive myself and everyone involved in abandoning me. I am thankful for all I have including *Who I Am*. As Spirit, I am *Love Power* and have all that I need to create a fulfilling relationship.

ACKNOWLEDGEMENT

BELIEF: I am not being acknowledged for the good I do. No matter what I do, I can't seem to please my partner. I am a failure - no good!

NEW THOUGHT: I acknowledge my own worth. The more I love myself, the easier it is for other people to accept, acknowledge and appreciate the good things I do.

ABUSE

BELIEF: I am not lovable. Whenever I get interested in someone who I think is special, that person starts using and hurting me. I need to protect myself from being hurt. Sometimes I am fearful for my safety.

NEW THOUGHT: I am loveable. Right *NOW,* I stop being a victim! It is my right to say what I want and to express my feelings. It is as easy to say *no* as it is to say *yes.* I say *no* whenever I need to stop someone from abusing me. I deserve to be listened to and heard. I am worthwhile. I choose not to be an enabler to someone who tries to abuse me; e.g, my partner.

ADDICTION

BELIEF: I rely on quick fixes (for example: alcohol, drugs, cigarettes, food, sex, excessive work, power and money, an inflated ego, feeling sorry for myself) to give me courage to handle my problems. Using quick fixes, I am able to endure my pain and fool myself into believing that everything is okay.

NEW THOUGHT: Here and now, I declare I am in control. When I feel an addictive craving coming on, I tell myself to *STOP* what I am thinking, and *CALM DOWN*. I focus my attention into a place of inner peace. From this place of inner peace, I create a step-by-step plan of action to guide me into new addictive-free experiences. I do whatever it takes to become the master of my thoughts and emotions.

AGE, COLOR, SEXUAL ORIENTATION, RELIGION, ATTRACTIVENESS

BELIEF: I am not good enough for a loving, lasting relationship so it won't work. I have one of these obstacles: not the right age (too big an age difference), not the right color, not the right sexual orientation, not the right religion, or not attractive enough. The relationship I want is destined to fail.

NEW THOUGHT: Love has no boundaries. As Kahil Gibran says in *The Prophet*, "Love if it finds you worthy, directs your course." *Love Power* overcomes every obstacle. I am worthy of a loving, lasting relationship and have faith it will work.

ANGER:

BELIEF: I am disgusted and prone to feelings of hate and even rage. I can't control what is happening. I blame other people, the situation, God, and fate. Deep down I am angry with myself because I do not know how to handle the situation.

NEW THOUGHT: I release and let go of my anger and other negative feelings by:

1. daily acknowledging the presence of my *Love Power*, and then breathing deeply into a feeling of calm where I can change my thoughts and feelings,

2. channeling my anger into an opportunity for positive inspiration and growth,

3. listening to the messages my anger gives me so I can change the way I perceive what is happening,

4. deliberately returning to love and trusting my *Love Power.*

ANXIETY/PERFORMANCE

BELIEF: I am overwhelmed by the thought of having to achieve my goals. They seem so big, and I fear I will be rejected if I don't accomplish them. I won't share my fears with my partner because I would appear weak and inadequate. I'll keep my performance anxiety to myself.

NEW THOUGHT: I deliberately move into a feeling of inner peace, awaken my *LOVE POWER,* and in the peace become mindful of my worthiness. Then, from a place of inner peace and worthiness, I break down my goals into small, achievable steps focusing on one step at a time. I share my hopes and fears with my partner. I accept and value myself for Who I Am.

ATTACHMENT

BELIEF: I am not able to separate my own worthiness from that of my partner. I am powerless to separate my own feelings and to express myself. I am easily hurt and defensive.

NEW THOUGHT: I emotionally stand out of the shadow of my partner and breathe deeply until I experience a calm sense of control and peace. This accomplished, I acknowledge my own abilities and strengths. I continue this practice until I am okay with or without my partner. I choose to be myself, to remember that I am important and that it is my responsibility to create my own happiness. The more fulfilled I am, the more love I have to share with my partner.

BEING BETRAYED

BELIEF: I am being betrayed and lied to. I hurt and don't like it.

NEW THOUGHT: Intentionally I forgive and move beyond the lie and any feelings of hurt and rejection. Instead, I reflect upon what I was thinking and doing that attracted my partner to betray me. I am willing to move into my *LOVE POWER* and change my thoughts to attract love, respect and acceptance.

BETRAYING OTHERS

BELIEF: I am not keeping my word. This way I am safe.

NEW THOUGHT: My word is my pledge and is sacred. Being truthful with my partner sets me free.

BEING CHEATED

BELIEF: My partner is either seeing someone else behind my back, or doing something about which I do know know and would disapprove. I can't trust my partner.

NEW THOUGHT: I openly share my thoughts and feelings with my partner, and am willing to understand my partner's thoughts and feelings. With compassion and good communication, we can resolve our issues. I faithfully do my *Love Communication* exercises.

BORED

BELIEF: My relationship with my partner is always the same – or, at least some part of it, is definitely boring. I must silently grin and bear the situation. There is nothing I can do to create excitement.

NEW THOUGHT: I open myself up to experiencing new things with or without my partner. I replace awkwardness, fear and perhaps shame with excitement and adventure. When stuck, I reach out and ask my partner for help. Being honest with my partner is my best tool.

BULLYING AND HURTING OTHERS

BELIEF: Bullying and hurting others is an effective way for me to be respected and get what I want. At a deep inner level bullying and hurting others helps me hide my own fears that I am not good enough and am not loved or loveable.

NEW THOUGHT: By believing in myself and embracing my *Love Power*, I can get what I want and be respected. I love and accept myself for Who I Am. Love, gratitude and kindness are effective ways of getting what I want and building a mutually fulfilling relationship. The only people who hurt are those people willing to be hurt. I can't make anyone hurt.

CHEATING ON MY PARTNER

BELIEF: I am cheating and being dishonest with my partner.

NEW THOUGHT: I have the strength and *Love Power* to be faithful and honest with my partner. Being honest and willing to forgive one another sets us both free.

COMMITMENT

BELIEF: I fear commitment. What if I pledge to love someone, and then my dreams are not fulfilled? I could end up being a prisoner in a relationship that I no longer want.

NEW THOUGHT: When I commit to a relationship, I choose to believe it will work. My pledge creates passion and is the driving

Love force of our intimacy. With commitment I gain freedom to share whom I am in an intimate relationship in which we both grow and prosper.

To achieve a relationship in which we both grow, I honour and respect myself and my partner for *whom we are*. As a way to nourish our self growth, I express my thoughts and feelings and lovingly listen to my partner. Whenever I experience we are not in harmony, I choose to communicate my concerns until we both return to feeling loved.

Fear is the lack of knowledge. With understanding and embracing my *Love Power*, fear will disappear.

COMPETITIVE

BELIEF: I will make it look as though I am as good as, or better than, anyone else. When my *fake me* is believed by others, I will relax. Nobody can love the *real me*.

NEW THOUGHT: I am worthwhile. By sharing our strengths and weaknesses, my partner and I are okay to make mistakes and trust we will continue to be loved for our *real selves*.

COMPLAINING

BELIEF: I can't get what I want unless I complain about what I don't like. My opinions matter.

NEW THOUGHT: By trusting my partner to listen to my desires, I get what I want. I focus positively on the future and ask for what I want. I make my requests reasonable, specific and something that I believe my partner can do.

CON ARTIST

BELIEF: If I tell my partner what he/she wants to hear, I can seduce my partner into getting what I want without having to reveal my own inadequacies. I fear telling my partner the truth.

NEW THOUGHT: Being honest with my partner sets me free. The more I love and trust myself, the more I am able to love and trust my partner. I am *Love Power* and am worthwhile.

DEFENSIVE/OVERBEARING/CONFRONTIVE

BELIEF: Reacting defensively and confronting others, I create a protective shield around me. This protects me from other people putting me down and from being a victim. It also makes me appear powerful. People would not like me if they knew the *real me.*

NEW THOUGHT: I am okay just the way I am. Other people's petty criticisms of me are a projection of who they are and have nothing to do with whom I am. I listen patiently to loving, constructive observations and expect my comments to be respectfully heard. I am filled with confidence. My *Love Power* sees me through.

DESERVING/INADEQUATE

BELIEF: I don't deserve an intimate lasting relationship. I am not worthy. Ultimately I ruin all my promising intimate relationships.

NEW THOUGHT: I deserve to be loved and to share an intimate lasting relationship. I am willing to work on all aspects of myself that I believe would not make me a good partner (e.g. a drug related addiction, anger issues, low self esteem). Deep down I know I am worthwhile. I love myself and am willing to receive. I am willing to share with my partner and go the extra mile to make our relationship work. Together we will let our *Love Power* shine.

DISAPPOINTMENT

BELIEF: I feel badly that what I want and expect in my relationship is not working. My partner is not doing what I want and what I believe is best for both of us.

NEW THOUGHT: I am willing to change my expectations and appreciate my partner for who he/she is. I trust we can overcome any obstacle by using our Love Power and communication tools wisely.

EMBARRASSED

BELIEF: I feel self-conscious and awkward exposing my thoughts and feelings.

NEW THOUGHT: It is okay to be vulnerable and to make mistakes. I love and trust myself. Being truthful with my partner sets us both free to be genuine and truly loved for who we are.

EMOTIONAL SHUT-DOWN

BELIEF: Not revealing my feelings enables me to be safe and avoid being hurt. Deep down I fear my attempts to get close will fail.

NEW THOUGHT: Sharing my thoughts and feelings with my partner brings us closer together. I choose to open my heart and trust the guidance of my Love Power to keep me safe.

FEAR

BELIEF: I place my faith in that which appears real, and then believe the worst could happen. Scared, I surrender my personal power to conditions outside myself that give me a false (fake) sense of security.

NEW THOUGHT: There is no barrier, no fears that our *Love Power* will not dissolve. With an open heart and mind, I embrace an attitude of love and gratitude. The light that shines forth from my *Love Power* casts out the dark shadows of fear until fear disappears. Love is the absence of fear. Fear is only a thought appearing real but has absolutely no validity - has no substance and is not real.

FORGIVENESS

> *You make what you defend against, and by*
> *your own defence against it, it is real*
> *and inescapable. Lay down your arms,*
> *and only then do you perceive it false.*

A Course in Miracles

BELIEF: I blame myself and sometimes others rather than forgiving. I act out of feelings of regret, hurt, anger, shame, guilt and remorse.

NEW THOUGHT: I forgive and choose thoughts that empower me to respect and appreciate myself and others. I am my own best friend. Everything I need to achieve satisfying relationships is within me. I am guided by and with my *Love Power.*

FRUSTRATION

BELIEF: I am blocked. I can't get what I want in my relationship. I feel like the saying, "I am damned if I do, and damned if I don't"

NEW THOUGHT: Being frustrated is okay because it motivates me to explore new solutions. When blocked, I like sharing my thoughts and feelings with my partner who is willing to listen and support me. I enjoy replacing worry, frustration and struggle with excitement to learn more and to grow. I trust my *Love Power.*

GUILT

BELIEF: I don't feel good about what I have done. It is my fault. I have violated my own code of ethics.

NEW THOUGHT: I forgive myself and release myself from feelings of guilt. By changing my thoughts, I change my experiences. The mistakes I make do not matter, but what I do to correct them does matter. The correction of my mistakes are my stepping stones to a happy, healthy relationship.

HEALTH CONCERNS

BELIEF: My health is poor. I don't want to be a burden.

NEW THOUGHT: I am a divine Spiritual Being having a human experience. My body is my intimate friend. I treat my body with respect. My thoughts create my experiences including my body, and not visa-versa. I *know* every day my health grows stronger.

HURTING/ FEAR OF BEING HURT

BELIEF: I have been hurt before and fear being hurt again. I am powerless and unable to defend myself against being hurt.

NEW THOUGHT: No one can hurt me unless I give them permission and accept being hurt. The more I love myself, the more my partner and other people are able to love me. I am willing to receive love. The past is gone, and every moment is a new opportunity to choose my thoughts and feelings wisely thus creating a new reality/ realization. Thank you, *Love Power!*

HYPOCONDRIAC

BELIEF: I worry about my health. I have no control over my health. I am limited by the belief that I have many physical ailments.

NEW THOUGHT: I am worthwhile. My body is my intimate friend and messenger. Thoughts are things and give me control over my health. My thoughts create my future including what happens in my body. I trust my *Love Power* to guide me in choosing thoughts that are good for my health.

INTELLECTUALIZING

BELIEF: I use my knowledge to create a rational defence that protects me from exposing my inadequacies and the possibility of being wrong. Deep down, I fear being exposed and rejected.

NEW THOUGHT: I am worthwhile. I let go of trying to protect myself from having to be right and instead trust in my Spiritual Essence to guide me. Sharing my real thoughts and feelings with my partner sets me free.

INTIMACY

BELIEF: I fear getting emotionally close and revealing my true thoughts and feelings. I don't want to be rejected, or to loose my freedom and feel useless.

NEW THOUGHT: My relationships mirror whom I am. By sharing an intimate relationship with my partner, we discover more about ourselves. This is an exciting adventure and way to grow the strength and beauty of who we are individually and as a couple. I believe Love is the strongest force in the universe and I can use my

Love Power to maintain a healthy, vibrant intimacy. Being truthful with my partner sets me free to deepen our intimacy.

JEALOUSY

BELIEF: My partner is mine and I expect my partner to be there exclusively for me. I am jealous and feel rage when my partner shows affection for someone else. Deep down, I am afraid my partner will leave me.

NEW THOUGHT: I believe I am worth loving and have the power to create what is best for me. If my partner were to choose someone else, I would honor my partner's decision. I would have faith that someone or something better for me would fill my emotional vacuum. I replace jealousy with love of myself, trust, and compassion.

JUDGEMENTAL/CRITICAL

BELIEF: What I believe is right. Usually I know what works and is good for other people including for my partner. It is my responsibility to set things right.

NEW THOUGHT: I am willing to see that what is right for me is often not what is right for other people including for my partner. As I focus on my partner's good qualities, we expand our understanding and appreciation of each other.

LONELINESS

BELIEF: I feel sad and empty being alone. I believe I am not worthy of being loved and am destined to remain alone. I experience deep loss in my lack of companionship.

NEW THOUGHT: Being alone provides me with an opportunity for self-discovery and to do things I could not do while being with a partner. I bless my alone time and being able to discover what I want in a lasting, intimate relationship. I move forward with confidence *knowing* I will attract my ideal relationship. I will make a list of all the attributes I desire and deserve (become the living compliment of what I am requesting), and put my request out to the law of the Universe *knowing* my ideal partner will be attracted to me.

LOSS

BELIEF: My relationships end up in loss due to death, divorce, rejection and/or abandonment. I fear being out of control and suffering emotional pain.

NEW THOUGHT: Loss is a reaction to experiences, and I no longer choose this reaction. Instead I choose thoughts of health, happiness and fulfilling relationships. I trust in a power of peace and love greater than myself to deliver what is best for me. I remember that my *Love Power* is part of the greatest force in the universe, and I can use it to attract a loving, lasting relationship.

MARRIAGE

BELIEF: Marriage is a romantic fairy tale of unrealistic expectations that don't come true. In my marriage I feel like the romance has died and I am stuck in a relationship where I can't get what I want. I have lost my freedom, don't know what to do, and am afraid of leaving. More than a third of marriages are either failing or not fulfilling.

NEW THOUGHT: I believe that love is the strongest force in the universe and that we can use Love Power. Using Love Power and good communication skills, my partner and I can make choices that are mutually fulfilling, enrich our lives, and bring us happiness. I focus on the large percentage of marriages that do succeed.

MATERIALISTIC

BELIEF: Money and material possessions give me power, prestige, and respect.

NEW THOUGHT: My happiness is being valued for whom I am. I open my heart and accept my inner peace as my power. This *Love Power* is the source and substance of my good experiences.

NARCISSISTIC/EGO DRIVEN

BELIEF: I am important, superior and deserve special recognition and treatment. When I don't get treated with special attention and loyalty, it is my job to criticize and belittle others like my partner. This way whomever I choose to criticize and belittle such as my partner can remember who is superior and whom they are serving. All people and events are an extension of me. I love myself and the world revolves around me.

NEW THOUGHT: I recognize that other people are separate from me and are important and special. I reach out to others including my partner with understanding, and recognize that I have a problem with insecurity. I focus on building a healthy self image. I put my faith and trust in a divine power greater than myself. I believe other people like my partner are there for me, and I am open to receiving their help.

OVERPROTECTIVE

BELIEF: My partner does not know what he/she is doing. I'll take care of my partner and protect him/her from potential harm.

Deep down, I am afraid that if my partner does not need me, I will be abandoned.

NEW THOUGHT: I am worthwhile. The more freedom I give my partner, the more freedom I receive. By trusting my partner and knowing my partner can take care of him/her self, I gain respect and deepen our intimacy.

OVERWHELMED

BELIEF: I feel out of control – swept up in a wave of pressure. I can't stay focused on doing what I want and don't believe my partner can or will help me. I keep making mistakes, am anxious, and fear our relationship is headed for disaster.

NEW THOUGHT: I do whatever it takes to relax. In a relaxed state I connect with my *Love Power*, Divine Essence, and ask Spirit to guide me - I am open to receiving and that includes help from my partner and other people. With trust and an open heart, I make plans breaking them into small manageable steps.

PAINFUL

BELIEF: Either I am in pain, or I can't stand to see my partner suffer. I can't figure out how to ask my partner for help and am not sure my partner would help if I asked. I feel helpless. The only way I know how to manage my pain is to avoid the sad situation.

NEW THOUGHT: There is no obstacle that enough *Love Power* can not overcome. By sharing with my partner and using professional skills if needed, we can heal any painful situation. Working together we deepen our understanding and intimacy. I choose to focus on a positive outcome, and to visualize myself and my partner in physical and emotional Well Being.

PLEASING MY PARTNER

BELIEF: I must do everything I can to please my partner or I won't be loved. Even if I have to go into sacrifice, I must please my partner.

NEW THOUGHT: Pleasing myself is as important as pleasing my partner. Together my partner and I share our intimate thoughts and feelings with the intention of both of us being pleased, happy and growing our relationship. We use our *Love Power* to guide us. We are grateful for our loving relationship, and all the blessings we have to share.

POWER STRUGGLE

BELIEF: I need to know I have power and to be in control of what happens in our relationship. It is important for me to be right. I need to defend myself as my partner tries to take control and win at being right.

NEW THOUGHT: I am powerful and get to choose how I use my power. Rather than trying to control what happens in our relationship and be right, I use my LOVE POWER and my communication skills to discover what my partner means – not just what my partner is saying. The more I love and appreciate my partner, the more I love and appreciate myself. I enjoy being an active partner in enhancing our intimacy.

PROCRASTINATION/EXCUSES

BELIEF: If I put off doing what I know I should do, I won't have to risk suffering unwanted consequences such as failure or more success than I can handle. By procrastinating, I can avoid taking responsibility for what happens. The thought of taking action is overwhelming.

NEW THOUGHT: As an individualized expression of the Divine, I exercise my God-given power of volition in choosing what to do, when, where and how. I enjoy taking small, incremental steps toward fulfillment. As I feel good about what I am doing, I attract successful experiences to me.

REJECTION

BELIEF: If I express my real thoughts and feelings, other people (including my partner) will reject me. I'll be abandoned, alone, and suffer pain in my loneliness. My dreams will be shattered.

NEW THOUGHT: I am worthwhile and worthy. Expressing my real thoughts and feelings attracts people (including my partner) who appreciate me for whom I am. I replace fear of being rejected with trust that I am worthwhile and provided for. When I am alone, I have the time to deepen and clarify what I truly want.

RESENTMENT

BELIEF: I am indignant and upset about what my partner is doing. I don't believe my partner wants to hear about what is upsetting me. Because I can't change what is happening, I have to put up with it. I will keep my anger to myself even though I know it is unhealthy to repress emotions.

NEW THOUGHT: I am in charge of my feelings and what happens to me. By trusting my partner, I can better understand the situation. I know my partner is willing to listen to my feelings. When we put love and our relationship first, we can share our thoughts and feelings and overcome any obstacle. We faithfully use our *Love Communication* knowledge and exercises.

RISK TAKING

BELIEF: I am afraid to risk taking action to better our relationship for fear that I will fail. If I fail, my partner may reject me and even leave me. I don't want to suffer hurting or being alone.

NEW THOUGHT: Love is letting go of fear. I am willing to use the power of love, *LOVE POWER,* to take risks and move through personal barriers. I am in control of my thoughts.

ROLE EXPECTATIONS

BELIEF: My parents, peers and culture taught me that men and women are supposed to act in certain ways. For example, men are supposed to be the performers and breadwinners, and women are supposed to be the housekeepers and manage the relationship. Men are expected to be strong and assertive, and women to be vulnerable and express their feelings. When I either can't or don't meet the male/female role expectations, I feel like a failure. I'm confused and frustrated.

NEW THOUGHT: It's okay to be different. I love myself just the way I am. Sharing my beliefs and feelings with my partner empowers my partner to love me for who I am.

"When men and women are able to respect
and accept their differences
then love has a chance to blossom."
—John Gray, "Men Are From Mars, *Women are From Venus"*

SAD/SORROWFUL

BELIEF: I feel sad things did not turn out as I believe they should have. Unfortunately there is nothing I can do about it. Sometimes I feel sad for other people, and sometimes I feel sad for myself.

NEW THOUGHT: I release myself from trying and judging the way things turned out. I accept that I can't change the past. I am worthy, powerful, and have the ability to make changes. My experiences provide me with an orderly sequence of learning and growth. As I focus on the present and future, I am 100% in charge of my present and future experiences.

SELF SACRIFICE

BELIEF: I must constantly give to my partner even if I am uncomfortable and sacrificing my own needs and desires. If I don't give enough, I will be criticized, rejected and jeopardize our intimacy.

NEW THOUGHT: Sharing what I need and desire with my partner frees me up to be myself and to receive. The more love I give, the more love I have to receive. When both my partner and I are happy, we unleash the power of our passion to bring us what we want joyously and to enjoy an authentic, trusting relationship..

SEX

BELIEF (For Men): If I do not perform well, I won't be loved by my partner. If my friends find out, they may laugh at me. Even at the expense of denying my own needs, I must please my partner.

BELIEF (For Women): If I don't act like I am happy and satisfied by my partner's love making, I will loose his love and affection.

NEW THOUGHT: Sex is one way I express my intimate love for my partner. Sharing both my fears and desires with my partner opens our hearts to be loved for who we are. I am patient, listen to what my partner wants, and am willing to explore new ways of sexual expression and making love.

SHAME

BELIEF: I or someone I know has intentionally broken a moral code of ethics and done something dishonorable, improper or hurtful. Being consciously aware of the event and what was happening, I suffer the pain of humiliation and embarrassment.

NEW THOUGHT: At a heart level, I am a good person. I forgive myself for my mistakes and forgive others for judging me. I move forward with kindness, confidence and a positive attitude.

SHY

BELIEF: Relationships are stressful and awkward for me in some situations. This includes the initial conversation, keeping the conversation going, expressing my feelings, and romance and sexuality. I feel inadequate and sometimes lack education. Deep down I do not feel worthy and believe I can easily be rejected.

NEW THOUGHT: I am worthwhile and loveable just the way I am. It is okay for me to ask for and receive help. Being truthful and asking questions puts my partner at ease and opens us up to share our strengths and weaknesses, and to deepen our intimacy.

STRESS

BELIEF: Mine or my partner's demands are more than I can

handle. It is hard to stay in control. Often I feel anxious, irritable, pressured, sick, depressed and tired.

NEW THOUGHT: A little stress motivates me. High stress controls me. When I experience high stress, I take a relaxation break. I relax until I experience a sense of inner peace that intuitively lets me know I am okay and choosing what to do. I am willing to break down my "to-do" lists into smaller steps, to ask for help (and that includes asking my partner), to use prayer, and also to use relaxation methods such as yoga and meditation.

STUBBORN

BELIEF: I am not going to listen to what my partner says. I'm not budging from my beliefs. No one can make me do what I don't want to do.

NEW THOUGHT: My partner and I are part of a larger spiritual whole. As I give to my partner, my partner is better equipped to please me. As I listen to my partner, I learn more about myself. I am willing to do whatever it takes to nourish our love and intimacy.

STUCKNESS

BELIEF: I am stuck in a repetitious pattern (such as rejection, addiction or abuse), and I can't get out.

NEW THOUGHT: Can't is another way of saying *I don't know how.* I open myself up to learning how to release myself from my stuck pattern – I am open to changing my thoughts, to meditation and prayer, to helpful information, and to professional coaching. I am patient and know a change in my thoughts/beliefs will change my experiences.

SUFFOCATING

BELIEF: I feel like life is slipping away from me and I am suffocating. I'm losing my identity and must sacrifice my beliefs to please and be loved. I lack faith in my own values and power.

NEW THOUGHT: Being stuck motivates me to re-examine my thoughts, beliefs and values. I refocus my thoughts from what I don't have to thoughts of gratitude for what I do have. I have faith that gratitude opens the doors for new and wonderful experiences to be attracted to me.

In an attitude of gratitude I give thanks for the following: "I am the source. I am the power. I am worthwhile and willing to express my beliefs. It is as easy to say *No* as it is to say *Yes.*"

TAKING YOUR PARTNER FOR GRANTED

BELIEF: (Please be aware that this belief is often held unconsciously.) Because my partner needs our relationship, I do not have to fear that my partner leaving me. By satisfying my partner's basic requirements, I am free to concentrate on other things I want.

NEW THOUGHT: As I listen to my partner's needs, it is easier to understand and appreciate my partner and myself. By sharing we create more freedom to live an authentic relationship in which we are free, mutually respected, and growing stronger. Focusing on my partner's good qualities expands our love. I enjoy sharing my intimate thoughts and feelings with my partner.

WITHDRAWAL

BELIEF: Withdrawing is my way of demonstrating my resignation and silently retaliating. I can appear mature and in control thus hiding my real anger and inability to know how to safely express myself.

NEW THOUGHT: I remember that I am LOVE POWER. Then, with calm courage, I forgive and reach out to understand my partner and the real meaning of what my partner is saying. To create an atmosphere of caring and safety, I find something my partner is doing that I like and with which I can agree. In a safe and caring atmosphere, we are empowered to share and use our communication skills. The more we share, the stronger our love and intimacy becomes.

CHAPTER SEVEN

A Touch Of Love

*"Our purpose in relationships is
to see that spirit of love in each other,
the light of love in everyone,
that is the only reality."*

—Gerald Jampolsky,
Out of the Darkness, Into the Light

When you feel that presence of love deep within your heart, you know you have made a spiritual connection. The Divine infinite supply that powers your love is working through you. This Truth is so profound that without question you know that you can trust your *Love Power*. It is an eternal force. Love is the most powerful force in the universe, and you can use it to create satisfying, loving relationships.

Peace goes hand-in-hand with your love feelings. Sometimes I imagine peace is like the fertile soil in my garden. When I plant a seed in my soil-of-peace, I imagine it growing into a flower like the delicate red rose – the fragrance and essence of which I take into my heart. As I cherish this red rose in my imagination, I know it will attract loving experiences.

Because we are all unique, there are thousands of different ways to attract loving experiences. To help you attract loving experiences that are perfect for you, I recommend that you relax with the following meditation and read the *Love Prayer* by Rev. Raymond Pilon at least once a day for 30 days. Embody the messages of the meditation and prayer until they feel like they are a part of Who You Are.

As a Thank You for completing the six week action program to achieve your *lasting relationship,* I offer you my meditation. Think of it as a touch of love from me to you.

Blenda's Meditation For Love

Please set aside 30 minutes of private
quiet time to enjoy your mediation.

Early morning and late evening are great times for meditating. Find a quiet space free of distractions, check that your phones are shut off, and make yourself comfortable. Invite that part of you that has chosen to do a meditation to relax.

When you are ready, begin by focusing your attention on your breath. Become aware of the rhythm of your breathing. Notice your breath slowing down, and relax as you continue to breathe in and breathe out. Allow your attention to move into the flow of the even rhythm of your breathing.

Next, invite your imagination to participate with you. Imagine your breath is massaging your gentle spirit. The longer your breath massages your spirit, the more deeply you experience the Oneness of your body, mind and spirit - Spirit, Divine Oneness! Relaxing even more deeply, entrust your Love Power to guide you.

As you continue to breathe in and out in a gentle rhythm, experience a pleasant sense of peace. Breathe into this peace by taking a deep breath. On the out-breath release a big sigh of relief from all the stress of the day. Then breathe in again and on the second out-breath release inner tension. With the third deep breath, on the out-breath release and let go of all trying. Experience yourself surrendering as you slowly move into a feeling of relaxed, harmonious peace. Take your time. Move gently as you settle into the sacred sanctuary of your peace.

When you intuitively know you are at peace, go back in your memory and recall an experience in which you felt loved and appreciated: perhaps lying in your mothers' arms, cuddling in your partner's arms, or when you did something special for someone and were appreciated. Take a couple of minutes to be present with these memories. Allow them to take you on a journey down memory lane. Recall only loving memories.

Continue breathing with a relaxed feeling of peace. Spend a couple of minutes enjoying your peace.

Become aware of how it feels to be at peace and loved. Experience the nurturing gentleness your thoughts are bringing you. Become aware of the depth of your breath and the slowness of your heartbeat. Observe if you feel a warm glow, or a tingling sensation moving throughout your body.

Continue to focus on the gentle feelings and as you observe them, describe how you know them. Are they warming your heart? Are they providing you a deep-seated feeling of peace? Welcome your gentle feelings. They are your friends letting you know you have arrived into the safety of you inner Divine sanctuary – a place where everything just *IS* - a sacred place where your secrets and vulnerabilities are safe.

Say, "Thank you gentle thoughts and feelings for being my friends and letting me know I am safe. I know my thoughts are protected."

Now allow your mind to recall an experience that *you would like to change*. Perhaps the experience happened when you were hurt as a child, abandoned by a lover, or criticized when you tried to do something good. As you focus on these memories, *keep the awareness alive of how you feel when you are having these thoughts...and at the same time recognize it is okay to have these feeling because you are safe and Divinely guided..*

Keep these safe feelings in the background of your attention and direct yourself to gradually move into past negative feelings such as anger, hurt, pain or rejection. Stay present in your uncomfortable feelings until they intuitively begin speaking to you. Open your heart and with your *Love Power,* imagine these feelings guiding you to know what you need to change. For convenience, let's name your negative feelings *Misery.*

Listen to *Misery*; treat *Misery* as your friend and listen to what *Misery* has to say to you. Send *Misery* loving thoughts. Say to *Misery*, "I know you are a part of me, and you are here for a reason. Tell me, what do you want? What is you purpose? Why you are here?"

Should these questions bring up painful feelings or memories, refocus on your peace and give peace permission to address your misery. Stand back and watch as your peace tells *Misery* that it is okay to feel awful. Have faith. Trust that your peace is a healer and is healing the pain of your *Misery* right now. Know that your peace is one with your Love Power.

Patiently wait until you observe some healing. Your healing may be small, or it may be big. Next, *return your attention to your love.* Again breathe into your peace, the peace that empowers your love. Feel your *Love Power* moving deep within. Feel this magnificent *Love Power* like the very air you breathe. It is everywhere, both inside and outside you – always available.

Relax and exhale three big sighs: a sigh of relief, of release and of letting go. Now, gradually move more deeply into your *LOVE POWER* - the power of love greater than yourself. Experience it as a positive, creative force within, around, and through you.

Using your imagination, light the inner passion of your love. Experience Love's power moving throughout your body, warming the tender strings of your heart. Know that all is well and you deserve to be loved.

Take your time. When you are ready, imagine reaching out and touching someone special with your love - this may be your partner, a friend, someone you want to forgive, or even your wounded inner child. Reach out and take this special person into the warmth of your heart. Wrap your arms around this special person and in a warm embrace tenderly say, "I love you! I love you! I love you!"

When you feel complete and the seed of your love is sown, release this special person. Trust in your Love Power. Let go of the seed you have sown. Let Love go and grow! Imagine this special person feeling loved and being happy. Imagine yourself feeling loved and being happy. Imagine all people feeling loved and being happy. Experience the force and power of your love.

Now say to yourself with authority, "I give thanks, and I know that within me there is a power of peace and love greater than myself. I accept this Love Power, and that it is available to me through my conscious choice. It is my loyal friend. *This power of love is my Love Power – my spiritual greatness.* It is the source of my love and happiness. I give thanks to my *Love Power.* I accept its power and presence."

I now breathe into my acceptance. I return my attention to my breath allowing it to guide me back into the room which I fill with the essence of my love. I am at peace knowing ...

I AM LOVE
ALL IS WELL IN MY WORLD RIGHT NOW!

To download the audio version of Blenda's MEDITATION FOR LOVE, go to the link: www.marriage-works.ca and go to the *Love Secrets* download.

Love Prayer

Here and now, in this moment, I declare the awesome presence of Creation, God, Spirit. I bring into my awareness this Allness: ONE! ONE! ONE! *Divine Creation* of all that is, and ever will be.

As I think, I bring into my experience loving, lasting relationships. I am the living embodiment of my thoughts.

Love shows the way, and Universal Law makes it possible. Here and now, in this moment, I use Universal Law. All I believe and embody becomes my reality because my thoughts and beliefs have activated this Law.

I am deeply honored and grateful for these Truths. I am deeply grateful for this knowledge and the manifestation of a loving, lasting relationship.

In my mind, I know this to be Divine Realization. I release my prayer ssurrendering it to Creation, God. Knowing my prayer is answered, I will think of this no more.

Thank you God. And, so *It* is done!

—Rev. Raymond J. Pilon, BA, CIMM, ordained minister

About the Author

For seventeen years in Vancouver, BC, Canada, Blenda enjoyed the private practice of Professional Clinical Therapy. Specializing in relationships, Blenda successfully worked with more than 6,500 clients. She brought into Canada the work of the renowned bestselling relationship author, Dr. John Gray and co-facilitated his relationship workshops. Later Dr. John Gray endorsed Blenda's book (see endorsements).

Having a strong interest in metaphysics, Blenda also became a minister. With her husband, Rev Raymond Pilon, they moved to Virginia Beach Virginia, where Blenda co-ministered in the *God Is One Center*. A few years after retiring from the ministry, Blenda and her husband traveled for ten years. As part of their adventure they fell in love with Costa Rica and remained there for eighteen months living fifty meters from the Caribbean Sea in what is often referred to as Paradise, "Pura Vida".

Eventually looking for more creativity than "Pura Vida" offered, the travellers returned to Canada. Blenda began helping people understand the magnificence of their LOVE POWER and wrote *Love Secrets, Falling in Love and Staying in Love*. Knowing the importance of discovering the secrets for achieving a loving and lasting intimacy, Blenda decided to offer her six week pre-marital and relationship course as well as private coaching sessions. Blenda delights in assisting couples to be happy, fulfilled, and flourish in a marriage-that-works.

Author, Blenda Pilon, was born in Jamestown, NY, and grew up in Westchester County, a suburb of NYC. In 1968 she graduated from Indiana University with an MSc in psychology, and later received a degree as a hypnotherapist from the American Society of Clinical Hypnosis. Blenda started off her career as a high school guidance counselor in Berwick, Pennsylvania. To become more aware of our changing world, Blenda briefly took a job as a guidance counselor in North Carolina some 40 years later.

As Blenda says, "What brings me the greatest satisfaction in my relationship work is seeing couples realize they are worthy of love and being loved, and that by using their *Love Power* they can enjoy the best relationship imaginable!"

Interested in learning more? Check out Blenda and her husband's exciting website!

www.marriage-works.ca

info@marriage-works.ca

www.marriage-works.ca

www.ingramcontent.com/pod-product-compliance
Lightning Source LLC
Chambersburg PA
CBHW052043090426
42739CB00010B/2034